THE ART OF WAR
IN THE MIDDLE AGES
A.D. 378-1515

BY $C.W.C.Oman$

REVISED AND EDITED

BY JOHN H. BEELER

D1051430

Cornell Paperbacks

CORNELL UNIVERSITY PRESS

ITHACA AND LONDON

First published, Oxford and London, 1885
Revised edition, published by permission, 1953,
by Cornell University Press
First printing, Great Seal Books, 1960
Second printing, 1963
Third printing, Cornell Paperbacks, 1968
Fourth printing, 1973

Published in the United Kingdom by Cornell University Press Ltd., 2-4 Brook Street, London W1Y 1AA

International Standard Book Number 0-8014-9062-6

Printed in the United States of America by Valley Offset, Inc.

Foreword

CARL LOTUS BECKER, perhaps more than any other American, made the study of history a force in the defense of our civilization against the physical and intellectual attacks of the totalitarian aggressors. If history is to maintain this position in the political and moral arena of today, it will be in large part through the development of the small books on large subjects of which Mr. Becker was both admirer and master. In these crowded times too few Americans, whether soldiers, scientists, statesmen, citizens, or students, can find the leisure to learn from the assimilated experience of the past through either monumental works or detailed monographs. The Cornell University Press is publishing this work in an effort to encourage and facilitate the publication of brief, well-written essays that will present the results of historical scholarship for the general reader.

The Art of War in the Middle Ages, written by the late C. W. C. Oman when he was still an undergraduate at Oxford, was awarded the Lothian Essay prize and was published in 1885. During a long and fruitful life of scholarship, the author dedicated himself to the development of the subject and subsequently published two major works under the same title. In spite of these, the original edition has been read so steadily that for some years it has been quite impossible to obtain even a secondhand copy. This new edition has been undertaken in the certain knowledge that the essay provides one of the very best pieces of collateral reading for the beginning student of mediaeval history and in the belief that, if available, it would find readers outside the college library. Dr. John H. Beeler accepted the task of incorporating the many points of factual information that have been established by more recent scholarship, because as a student of mediaeval warfare he recognized the intrinsic quality of the essay and as a member of the staff of a large introductory history course he had discovered its usefulness in leading the beginner beyond the confines of a required text.

EDWARD W. FOX

Preface

IN THE hands of modern historians, the military aspects of mediaeval society have suffered a strange neglect. References to the art of war may occasionally be dug out of obscure corners in general narratives. But in spite of the fact that war, perhaps more than religion and only less than agriculture, dominated the daily life of western Europe during the centuries intervening between the disappearance of the Roman Empire and the emergence of modern states, the subject has largely been left to novelists and antiquarians. The mediaeval knight has come down to us as a great fighter but an incompetent soldier, and the chronicles of his campaigns have been treated as quaint misrepresentations of unimportant actions. For an age such as ours, which is facing the problem of adjusting its social relations and political theories to new and revolutionary developments in the art of war, the history of warfare in the Middle Ages should provide a profitable field of study. The account that follows—a revision of C. W. C. Oman's essay of 1884—was the first attempt to

survey the whole broad field of warfare, and it has remained one of the best accounts available to the general
reader. Revision has been necessary only in a few places
where subsequent scholarship, often that of the author
himself, has substantially changed our understanding of
specific events. Occasionally, a sentence or a phrase has
been deleted, but wherever the author's wording has been
altered, the passage has been set off in brackets. No further
explanation has been provided except for the few extended
sections that have been completely rewritten, and, for
these, references to the sources have been provided in footnotes. For the rest, the text is reprinted as it originally appeared.

Unfortunately, no good bibliography of mediaeval military history exists in English, but it is hoped the succeeding paragraphs will provide those whose interest may be
aroused by this account with sufficient bibliographical
data to enable them to follow their interest into more
specialized areas. The *Cambridge Mediaeval History*
bibliographies for A. H. Thompson's "The Art of War to
1400" (vol. VI, chap. xxiii) and Sir Charles Oman's "The
Art of War in the Fifteenth Century" (vol. VIII, chap.
xxi) are the best available. Wilhelm Erben's *Kriegsge-
schichte des Mittelalters* (Beiheft 16 of *Historischen Zeit-
schrift*, 1929) contains a very useful bibliography for students who are able to use German. Specialized bibliographies will be mentioned in connection with the publications
on each topic.

A monopoly on the general subject of war in the Middle Ages has long been held by Professor, later Sir, Charles
Oman. His Lothian Prize Essay of 1884, which was published the following year as *The Art of War in the Middle*

Ages (Oxford, 1885) and is being reissued in this volume, ran through two subsequent and much-expanded versions. The first, *A History of the Art of War in the Middle Ages* (London, 1898), carried the history of mediaeval warfare only as far as the latter part of the fourteenth century, and the second, *A History of the Art of War in the Middle Ages* (London, 1924), a two-volume edition, extended the narrative to the end of the fifteenth century. These are the only general works on the subject now available in English, and they have the admirable quality of being eminently readable. Lynn Montross, whose *War through the Ages* (New York, 1944) contains a short, general bibliography, is the only recent author to include an account of the Middle Ages in a general work of military history. Mr. Montross leans heavily upon Professor Oman, and though he contributed nothing new to an understanding of the period, his style is highly entertaining. In addition, two European scholars must be mentioned. Hans Delbrück in the third volume of his learned *Geschichte des Kriegskunst im Rahmen des politische Geschichte* (Berlin, 1907) deals entirely with warfare in the Middle Ages. Professor Delbrück is chiefly remembered as one of the early twentieth-century scholars who did much to establish the unreliability of mediaeval numbers. More recently Ferdinand Lot published a two-volume work, *L'Art militaire et les armées au moyen age* (Paris, 1949), which is of tremendous importance to the student of continental military history. For English affairs, however, he based his work on Oman's 1898 edition, and consequently it is of little value for this field.

Among the problems that vex the mediaevalist, none is so thorny as the problem of numbers. How great was the income of kings? How large were their armies? Mediaeval annals are full of answers that were generally accepted as reasonably accurate until about the turn of the century. Dr. Delbrück's pamphlet *Numbers in History* (London, 1913) and, from a more strictly military point of view, J. H. Ramsey's "The Strength of English Armies in the Middle Ages," *English Historical Review*, XXIX (April, 1914), will help the casual reader to a better understanding of the problem.

Among books usually obtainable, those devoted to the wars of the English naturally predominate. *Warfare in England* (London, [n.d.]), by Hilaire Belloc, is a short, popular account of military events in England from the time of Caesar to the last Jacobite rising in 1745. From the scholarly point of view, the best account of any single phase of mediaeval English warfare is John E. Morris' *The Welsh Wars of King Edward the First* (Oxford, 1901). For keen historical analysis and thorough documentation, it is a model of its kind. The sources for the reconstruction of most mediaeval battles is scanty at best. The problem of interpreting these fragmentary remains has frequently given rise to heated arguments among historians. One of the great demolishers of other men's theories was the late J. H. Round, and students of military history can do no better than to read his classic study of "Mr. Freeman and the Battle of Hastings," in *Feudal England* (London, 1895). On a less polemical level are two works on the controversial phases of the battle of Bannockburn, *The Battle of Bannockburn* (Glasgow, 1913) by W. M. MacKenzie and John E. Morris' *Bannockburn* (Cambridge, 1914). These should be read in conjunction since, incorporating the best of modern historical research and writing, they show the divergences not only of the independent work but also of the national prejudices of two individuals, Mr. MacKenzie, the Scot, and Mr. Morris, the Englishman.

The military scene in the Middle Ages was profoundly affected by the architectural development of the castle. A short description of the mediaeval castle, with an extensive bibliography, is to be found in "Military Architecture," by A. Hamilton Thompson, in the *Cambridge Mediaeval History* (vol. VI, chap. xxii). An excellent account is Sidney Toy's *Castles: A Short History of Fortification from 1600 B.C. to A.D. 1600* (London, 1939). This is the only general history of military architecture in English. On the narrower stage of England, a number of good books are available. Out of date, but still a classic, is *Mediaeval Military Architecture in England* (London, 1884, 2 vols.), by George T. Clark. Mr. Clark was an engineer and not a historian, and some of his theories went rather wide of the mark; but he laid the groundwork for all subsequent investigation. Round's "Castles of the Conquest," *Archaeologia*, LVII (1902), exposed Clark's shortcomings, and this article was followed by Ella Armitage's *The Early Norman Castles of the British Isles* (London, 1912), which is still the definitive work on the origin of the castle in England. *Military Architecture in England during the Middle Ages* (London, 1912) by A. Hamilton Thompson is an account of the architectural development of English fortifications until the close of the Middle Ages and contains a good bibliography. *Castles* (London, 1926) by Sir Charles Oman and *The English Castle* (2d ed., rev.; London, 1932) by Hugh Braun are two popular descriptions. Mr. Braun is an archaeologist whose articles appear regularly in the leading English archaeological journals. His opinion may be regarded as representing the best contemporary ideas on the subject of castles. Other books on castles are William Douglas Simpson's *Castles from the Air* (London and New York, 1949), William Mackay Mackenzie's *The Mediaeval Castle in Scotland* (London, 1927), and Harold G. Leask's *Irish Castles and Castellated Houses* (Dundalk, Ireland, 1941).

The armor in which men fought and the weapons with which they fought had a definite relationship to the tactics of mediaeval warfare. *Armour and Weapons* (Oxford, 1909) by Charles Ffoulkes is a brief, well-illustrated general account, with a short but useful bibliography. Longer and consequently more detailed is Charles Ashdown's *British and Foreign Arms and Armour* (London, 1909), which is also excellently illustrated. *Armour and Weapons in the Middle Ages* (London, 1925) by the same author contains a short bibliography and a most useful glossary of armorial nomenclature.

The sources for the study of mediaeval warfare are concealed in the chronicles, the charters, and the official records of the period. The casual student will have little occasion to consult them, and the reader whose interest will have been stimulated by the following essay, it is hoped, will find enough clues to allow his interest to lead him in whatever direction it will.

JOHN H. BEELER

Greensboro, N.C.
April, 1953

Introduction

THE art of war has been very simply defined as "the art which enables any commander to worst the forces opposed to him." It is therefore conversant with an enormous variety of subjects: strategy and tactics are but two of the more important of its branches. Besides dealing with discipline, organization, and armament, it is bound to investigate every means which can be adapted to increase the physical or moral efficiency of an army. The author who opened his work with a dissertation on "the age which is preferable in a generalissimo," or "the average height which the infantry soldier should attain," [1] was dealing with the art of war, no less than he who confined himself to purely tactical speculations.

The complicated nature of the subject being taken into consideration, it is evident that a complete sketch of the social and political history of any period would be neces-

[1] Flavius Vegetius Renatus, *Military Institutions of the Romans*, tr. John Clark (Harrisburg, Penna., 1944), p. 15; Maurice, *Artis militaris*, ed. J. Scheffer (Upsala, 1664).

sary to account fully for the state of the "art of war" at the time. That art has existed, in a rudimentary form, ever since the day on which two bodies of men first met in anger to settle a dispute by the arbitrament of force. At some epochs, however, military and social history have been far more closely bound up than at others. There have been times when the whole national organization was founded on the supposition of a normal state of strife. In such cases the history of the race and of its "art of war" are one and the same. To detail the constitution of Sparta, or of ancient Germany, is to give little more than a list of military institutions. Conversely, to speak of the characteristics of their military science involves the mention of many of their political institutions.

At no time was this interpenetration more complete than in the age which forms the central part of our period. Feudalism, in its origin and development, had a military as well as a social side, and its decline was by no means unaffected by military considerations. There is a point of view from which its history could be described as "the rise, supremacy, and decline of heavy cavalry as the chief power in war." To a certain extent the tracing out of this thesis will form the subject of our researches. It is here that we find the thread which links the history of the military art in the Middle Ages into a connected whole. Between Adrianople (A.D. 378), the first, and Marignano (A.D. 1515), the last of the triumphs of the mediaeval horseman, lie the chapters in the scientific history of war which we are about to investigate.

Contents

CHAPTER III: *Page 31*

The Byzantines and Their Enemies (A.D. *582–1071*)

Character of Byzantine Strategy

Arms, Organization, and Tactics of the Byzantine Armies

CHAPTER IV: *Page 57*

The Supremacy of Feudal Cavalry (A.D. *1066–1346*)

CHAPTER VII: *Page 152*

Conclusion

CHRONOLOGICAL LIST OF BATTLES: *Page 167*

INDEX: *Page 171*

CHAPTER I

The Transition from Roman to Mediaeval Forms in War

A.D. 378-582

FROM THE BATTLE OF ADRIANOPLE
TO THE ACCESSION OF MAURICE

BETWEEN the middle of the fourth and the end of the sixth century lies a period of transition in military history, an epoch of transformations as strange and as complete as those political and economic changes [which turned European civilization into new channels of modern history.] * In war, as in all else, the institutions of the ancient world were seen to pass away and a new order of things to emerge.

Numerous and striking as are the symptoms of that period of tradition, none is more characteristic than the gradual disuse of the honored name of "legion," the title intimately bound up with all the ages of Roman greatness. The name indeed survived throughout the greater part of

---

* In all cases, changes in the wording of the original essay have been indicated by brackets. Attention is called to major revisions by footnotes, but this has not been thought necessary in the case of minor changes.—EDITOR

1

the fifth century, but by Justinian's time it had become obsolete. And with the name, the characteristic form of military efficiency which it had represented vanished. That wonderful combination of strength and flexibility, so solid and yet so agile and facile to maneuver, had ceased to correspond to the needs of the time. Sword and pilum had given place to lance and bow. The typical Roman soldier was no longer the iron legionary who, with shield fitted close to his left shoulder and sword hilt sunk low, cut his way through the thickest hedge of pikes, and stood firm before the wildest onset of Celt or German.[1] The organization of Augustus and Trajan was swept away by Constantine, and the legions which for three hundred years had preserved their identity, their proud titles of honor, and their *esprit de corps* knew themselves no longer.[2]

Constantine, when he cut down the numbers of the military unit to a quarter of its former strength and created many scores of new corps,[3] was acting from motives of political and not military expediency. The armament and general character of the troops survived their organization, and the infantry, the *robur peditum,* still remained the most important and numerous part of the army. At the same time, however, a tendency to strengthen the calvary made itself felt, and the proportion of that arm to the whole number of the military establishment continued steadily to increase

[1] P. Cornelius Tacitus, *Annals,* Bk. II, 21, in *The Complete Works of Tacitus,* ed. Moses Hadas (New York, 1942), p. 64.

[2] The old legions of the first century are found in full vigor at the end of the third. The coins of the British usurper Carausius commemorate as serving under him several of the legions which, as early as the reign of Claudius, were already stationed in Britain and Gaul.

[3] He had 132 legions and *numeri,* besides 100 unattached cohorts.

throughout the fourth century. Constantine himself, by depriving the legion of its complementary *turmae* and uniting the horsemen into larger independent bodies, bore witness to their growing importance. It would seem that the empire —having finally abandoned the offensive in war and having resolved to confine itself to the protection of its own provinces—found that there was an increasing need for troops who could transfer themselves with rapidity from one menaced point on the frontier to another. The Germans could easily distance the legion, burdened by the care of its military machines and impedimenta. Hence cavalry in larger numbers was required to intercept their raids.

But it would appear that another reason for the increase of the horsemen was even more powerful. The ascendancy of the Roman infantry over its enemies was no longer so marked as in earlier ages, and it therefore required to be more strongly supported by cavalry than had been previously necessary. The Franks, Burgundians, and Alamanni of the days of Constantine were no longer the half-armed savages of the first century, who, "without helm or mail, with weak shields of wickerwork, and armed only with the javelin," tried to face the embattled front of the cohort. They had now the ironbound buckler, the pike, and the short stabbing sword (scramasax), as well as the long cutting sword (spatha) and the deadly francisca or battle-ax, which, whether thrown or wielded, would penetrate Roman armor and split the Roman shield. As weapons for hand-to-hand combat these so far surpassed the old framea that the imperial infantry found it no light matter to defeat a German tribe. At the same time, the morale of the Roman army was no longer what it had once been: the corps were no longer homogeneous, and the insufficient supply of recruits was eked out by enlisting slaves and barbarians in the legions themselves, and not only among the auxiliary cohorts. Though seldom wanting in courage, the troops of the fourth century had lost the self-reliance and cohesion of the old Roman infantry, and required far more careful handling on the part of the general.

This tendency to deterioration on the part of the Roman infantry and the consequent neglect of that arm by the generals of the time were brought to a head by a disaster. The battle of Adrianople (A.D. 378) was the most fearful defeat suffered by a Roman army since Cannae (216 B.C.), a slaughter to which it is aptly compared by the military author Ammianus Marcellinus. The emperor Valens, all his chief officers,[4] and forty thousand men were left upon the field; indeed the army of the East was almost annihilated, and was never reorganized upon the same lines as had previously served for it.

The military importance of Adrianople was unmistakable; it was a victory of cavalry over infantry. The imperial army had developed its attack on the barricaded camp of the Goths, and the two forces were hotly engaged, when suddenly a great body of horsemen charged in upon the Roman left flank. It was the main strength of the Gothic cavalry, which had been foraging at a distance; receiving news of the fight it had ridden straight for the battlefield. Two of Valens' squadrons, which covered the flank of his array, threw themselves in the way of the oncoming mass and were ridden down and trampled under foot. Then the Goths swept down on the infantry of the left wing, rolled

[4] The Grand Masters of the infantry and cavalry, the Count of the Palace, and 35 commanders of different corps. Ferdinand Lot, *L'Art militaire,* I, 25, finds these figures incredible.

it up, and drove it in upon the center. So tremendous was their impact that the legions and cohorts were pushed together in helpless confusion. Every attempt to stand firm failed, and in a few minutes left, center, and reserve were one indistinguishable mass. Imperial guards, light troops, lancers, *foederati,* and infantry of the line were wedged together in a press that grew closer every moment. The Roman cavalry saw that the day was lost, and rode off without another effort. Then the abandoned infantry realized the horror of their position: equally unable to deploy or to fly, they had to stand to be cut down. It was a sight such as had been seen once before at Cannae, and was to be seen once after at Roosebeke (A.D. 1382). Men could not raise their arms to strike a blow, so closely were they packed; spears snapped right and left, their bearers being unable to lift them to a vertical position; many soldiers were stifled in the press. Into this quivering mass the Goths rode, plying lance and sword against the helpless enemy. It was not till two-thirds of the Roman army had fallen that the thinning of the ranks enabled a few thousand men to break out [5] and follow their right wing and cavalry in a headlong flight.

Such was the battle of Adrianople, the first great victory gained by that heavy cavalry which had now shown its ability to supplant the heavy infantry of Rome as the ruling power of war. During their sojourn in the steppes of southern Russia the Goths, first of all Teutonic races, had become a nation of horsemen. Dwelling in the Ukraine, they had felt the influence of that land, ever the nurse of cavalry, from the day of the Scythian to that of the Tartar and Cossack. They had come to "consider it more honourable to

---

[5] Ammianus Marcellinus, *Roman History,* tr. C. D. Yonge (London, 1894), pp. 608–615.

fight on horse than on foot," [6] and every chief was followed
by his war band of mounted men. Driven against their will
into conflict with the empire, they found themselves face
to face with the army that had so long held the world in
fear. The shock came, and, probably to his own surprise,
the Goth found that his stout lance and good steed would
carry him through the serried ranks of the legion. He had
become the arbiter of war, the lineal ancestor of all the
knights of the Middle Ages, the inaugurator of that ascendancy of the horseman which was to endure for a thousand
years.

Theodosius, on whom developed the task of reorganizing
the troops of the Eastern Empire, appears to have appreci-
ated to its fullest extent the military meaning of the fight
of Adrianople. Abandoning the old Roman theory of war,
he decided that the cavalry must in future compose the
most important part of the imperial army. To provide himself with a sufficient force of horsemen, he was driven to a
measure destined to sever all continuity between the military organization of the fourth and that of the fifth century.
He did not, like Constantine, raise new corps, but began
to enlist wholesale every Teutonic chief whom he could
bribe to enter his service. The war bands which followed
these princes were not incorporated with the national
troops; they obeyed their immediate commanders alone,
and were strangers to the discipline of the Roman army.
Yet to them was practically entrusted the fate of the empire, since they formed the most efficient division of the
imperial forces. From the time of Theodosius the prince had
to rely for the maintenance of order in the Roman world
merely on the amount of loyalty which a constant stream

[6] Maurice, *Artis militaris*, Lib. VI.

of titles and honors could win from the commanders of the *foederati*.

Only six years after Adrianople there were already 40,000 Gothic and other Teutonic horsemen serving under their own chiefs in the army of the east. The native troops sank at once to an inferior position in the eyes of Roman generals, and the justice of their decision was verified a few years later when Theodosius' German mercenaries won for him the two well-contested battles which crushed the usurper Magnus Maximus and his son Victor. On both those occasions the Roman infantry of the west, those Gallic legions who had always been considered the best footmen in the world, were finally ridden down by the Teutonic cavalry who followed the standard of the legitimate emperor.[7]

A picture of the state of the imperial army in the western provinces, drawn precisely at this period, has been preserved for us in the work of Vegetius, a writer whose treatise would be of far greater value had he refrained from the attempt to identify the organization of his own day with that of the first century by the use of the same words for entirely different things. In drawing inferences from his statements, it has also to be remembered that he frequently gives the ideal military forms of his imagination, instead of those which really existed in his day. For example, his legion is made to consist of 6,000 men, while we know that at the end of the fourth century its establishment did not exceed 1,500. His work is dedicated to one of the emperors

[7] At the still fiercer fight where the army of the usurper Eugenius almost defeated Theodosius, we find that it was the barbarian cavalry of Arbogast, not the native infantry, which had become (only seven years after Maximus' defeat) the chief force of the western empire.

who bore the name of Valentinian, probably to the second, as (in spite of Gibbon's arguments in favor of Valentinian III) the relations of the various arms to each other and the character of their organization point to a date prior to the commencement of the fifth century.

A single fact mentioned by Vegetius gives us the date at which the continuity of the existence of the old Roman heavy infantry may be said to terminate. As might be expected, this epoch exactly corresponds with that of the similar change in the east, which followed the battle of Adrianople. The tactician says:

From the foundation of the city to the reign of the sainted Gratian, the legionaries wore helmet and cuirass. But when the practice of holding frequent reviews and sham-fights ceased, these arms began to seem heavy, because the soldiers seldom put them on. They therefore begged from the emperor permission to discard first their cuirasses, and then even their helmets, and went to face the barbarians unprotected by defensive arms. In spite of the disasters which have since ensued, the infantry have not yet resumed the use of them. . . . And now, how can the Roman soldier expect victory, when helmless and unarmoured, and even without a shield (for the shield cannot be used in conjunction with the bow), he goes against the enemy? [8]

Vegetius—often more of a rhetorician than a soldier—has evidently misstated the reason of this change in infantry equipment. At a time when cavalry were clothing themselves in more complete armor, it is not likely that the infantry were discarding it from mere sloth and feebleness. The real meaning of the change was that, in despair of resisting horsemen any longer by the solidity of a line of

[8] Flavius Vegetius Renatus, *Military Institutions of the Romans,* tr. John Clark (Harrisburg, Penna., 1944), pp. 24, 38–39, 90.

heavy infantry, the Romans had turned their attention to the use of missile weapons—a method of resisting cavalry even more efficacious than that which they abandoned, as was to be shown a thousand years later at Crécy and Agincourt. That Vegetius' account is also considerably exaggerated is shown by his enumeration of the legionary order of his own day, where the first rank was composed of men retaining shield, pilum, and cuirass (whom he pedantically calls *Principes*). The second rank was composed of archers who wore the cuirass and carried a lance also; only the remaining half of the legion had entirely discarded armor and given up all weapons but the bow.

Vegetius makes it evident that cavalry, though its importance was rapidly increasing, had not yet entirely supplanted infantry to such a large extent as in the eastern empire. Though no army can hope for success without them, and though they must always be at hand to protect the flanks, they are not, in his estimation, the most effective force. As an antiquary he feels attached to the old Roman organization, and must indeed have been somewhat behind the military experience of his day. It may, however, be remembered that the Franks and Alamanni, the chief foes against whom the western legions had to contend, were—unlike the Goths—nearly all footmen. [It was not until the time of Alaric that Rome made the acquaintance of the Gothic horsemen, whom Constantinople had already met and for the moment contrived to buy off. In the days of Honorius, however, the Goth became the terror of Italy, as he had previously been of the Balkan Peninsula. His lance and steed once more asserted their supremacy: the generalship of Stilicho, the regular infantry of the old Roman army, and the native and *foederate* squadrons whose array flanked the legions were insufficient to arrest the Gothic charge. For years the conquerors rode at their will through Italy, and when they quit it in A.D. 409, it was by their own choice. There were no troops left in the western world who could have expelled them by force of arms.]

The day of infantry had in fact gone by in southern Europe; they continued to exist, not as the core and strength of the army, but for various minor purposes—to garrison towns or operate in mountainous countries. Roman and barbarian alike threw their vigor into the organization of their cavalry. Even the duty of acting as light troops fell into the hands of the horsemen. The Roman trooper added the bow to his equipment, and in the fifth century the native force of the empire had come to resemble that of its old enemy, the Parthian state of the first century, being composed of horsemen armed with bow and lance. Mixed with these horse archers fought squadrons of the *foederati*, armed with the lance alone. Such were the troops of Aëtius and Ricimer, the army which faced the Huns on the plain of Châlons (A.D. 451).

The Huns themselves were another manifestation of the strength of cavalry, formidable by their numbers, their rapidity of movement, and the constant rain of arrows which they would pour in without allowing their enemy to close. In their tactics they were the prototypes of the hordes of Alp Arslan, of Genghis, and Tamerlane. But mixed with the Huns in the train of Attila marched many subject German tribes, Herules and Gepids, Scyri, Lombards, and Rugians, akin to the Goths alike in their race and their manner of fighting. Châlons, then, was fought by horse archer and lancer against horse archer and lancer, a fair conflict with equal weapons. The Frankish allies of Aëtius were by far the most important body of infantry on the field, and these were ranged, according to the traditional tactics of Rome, in the center—flanked on one side by the Visigothic lances, on the other by the imperial array of horse archers and heavy cavalry intermixed. The victory was won not by superior tactics but by sheer hard fighting, the decisive point having been the riding down of the native Huns by Theodoric's heavier horsemen.

To trace out in detail the military meaning of all the wars of the fifth century does not fall within our province. As to the organization of the Roman armies a few words will suffice. In the west the *foederati* became the sole force of the empire, so that at last one of their chiefs, breaking through the old spell of the Roman name, could make himself, in title as well as in reality, ruler of Italy. In the east, the decline of the native troops never reached this depth. Leo I (A.D. 457–474), taking warning from the fate of the western empire, determined to increase the proportion of Romans to *foederati*, and carried out his purpose, though it cost the life of his benefactor, the Gothic patrician Aspar. Zeno (A.D. 474–491) continued this work, and made himself noteworthy as the first emperor who utilized the military virtues of the Isaurians, or semi-Romanized mountaineers of the interior of Asia Minor. Not only did they form his imperial guard, but a considerable number of new corps were raised among them. Zeno also enlisted Armenians and other inhabitants of the Roman frontier of the east, and handed over to his successor, Anastasius, an army in which the barbarian element was adequately counterpoised by native troops. [He had also rendered the empire an excellent turn by inducing the Ostrogoths, his nearest and most dangerous Teutonic neighbors, to migrate to Italy.]

The victorious armies of Justinian were therefore composed of two distinct elements, the foreign auxiliaries, serving under their own chiefs, and the regular imperial troops. The pages of Procopius give us sufficient evidence that in both these divisions the cavalry was by far the most important arm. The light horseman of the Asiatic provinces wins his especial praise. With body and limbs clothed in mail, his quiver at his right side and his sword at his left, the Roman trooper would gallop along and discharge his arrows to front or flank or rear with equal ease. The heavier squadrons of the subsidized Lombard, or Herule, or Gepidan princes, armed with the lance, marched in the second line to support him. "There are some," writes Procopius, "who regard antiquity with wonder and respect, and attach no special worth to our modern military institutions: it is, however, by means of the latter that the weightiest and most striking results have been obtained." [9] The men of the sixth century were, in fact, entirely satisfied with the system of cavalry tactics which they had adopted, and looked with a certain air of superiority on the infantry tactics of their Roman predecessors.

Justinian's army and its achievements were indeed worthy of all praise; its victories were its own, while its defeats were generally due to the wretched policy of the emperor, who persisted in dividing up the command among many hands—a system which secured military obedience at the expense of military efficiency. Justinian might, however, plead in his defense that the organization of the army had become such that it constituted a standing menace to the central power. The system of the Teutonic *comitatus,*

[9] Procopius, *De Bello Persico* in *Corpus Scriptorum Historiae Byzantinae* (Bonn, 1833), preface.

of the war band surrounding a leader to whom the soldiers were bound by a personal tie, had become deeply ingrained in the imperial forces. Always predominant among the *foederati,* it had spread from them to the native corps. In the sixth century the monarch had always to dread that the loyalty of the troops toward their immediate commanders might prevail over their higher duties. Belisarius and even Narses were surrounded by large bodyguards of chosen men, bound to them by oath. That of the former general at the time of his Gothic triumph amounted to 7,000 veteran horsemen. The existence of such corps rendered every successful commander a possible Wallenstein, to use a name of more modern importance. Thus the emperor, in his desire to avert the predominance of any single officer, would join several men of discordant views in the command of an army, and usually ensure the most disastrous consequences. This organization of the imperial force in *banda,*[10] bodies attached by personal ties to their leaders, is the characteristic military form of the sixth century. Its normal prevalence is shown by the contemporary custom of speaking of each corps by the name of its commanding officer, and not by any official title. Nothing could be more opposed than this usage to old Roman precedent.

The efficiency of Justinian's army in the Vandalic, Persian, or Gothic wars depended (as has already been implied) almost entirely on the combination of archers and heavy cavalry. The troops, whether Teutonic or eastern, against which it was employed were also horsemen. Engaging them the Romans prevailed, because in each case they were able to meet their adversaries' weapons and tactics not merely with similar methods, but with a greater

[10] This Teutonic word was in full acceptance in the sixth century.

variety of resources. Against the Persian horse archer were sent not only the light cavalry equipped with arms of the same description, but the heavy *foederate* lancers, who could ride the Oriental down. Against the Gothic heavy cavalry the same lancers were supported by the mounted bowmen, to whom the Goths had nothing to oppose. If, however, the Roman army enjoyed all the advantages of its diverse composition, it was, on the other hand, liable to all the perils which arise from a want of homogeneity. Its various elements were kept together only by military pride, or confidence in some successful general. Hence, in the troublous times which commenced in the end of Justinian's reign and continued through those of his successors, the whole military organization of the empire began to crumble away. A change not less sweeping than that which Theodosius had introduced was again to be taken in hand. In A.D. 582 the reforming emperor Maurice came to the throne and commenced to recast the imperial army in a new mold.

CHAPTER II

The Early Middle Ages

A.D. 476—1066-1081

FROM THE FALL OF THE WESTERN EMPIRE
TO THE BATTLES OF HASTINGS AND DURAZZO

The Franks, Anglo-Saxons, Scandinavians, etc.

IN LEAVING the discussion of the military art of the later Romans in order to investigate that of the nations of northern and western Europe, we are stepping from a region of comparative light into one of doubt and obscurity. The data which in the history of the empire may occasionally seem scanty and insufficient are in the history of the Teutonic races often entirely wanting. To draw from the fragmentary authorities an estimate of the military importance of the eastern campaigns of Heraclius is not easy, but to discover what were the particular military causes which settled the event of the day at Vouglé (A.D. 507) or Tolbiacum (ca. A.D. 510), at Badbury (ca. A.D. 900) or the Heavenfield (A.D. 634), is absolutely impossible. The state of the art of war in the Dark Ages has to be worked out from monkish chronicles and national songs, from the casual references of Byzantine historians, from the quaint drawings of the illuminated manuscript, or the moldering fragments found in the warrior's barrow.

It is fortunate that the general characteristics of the period render its military history comparatively simple. Of strategy there could be little in an age when men strove to win their ends by hard fighting rather than by skillful operations or the utilizing of extraneous advantages. Tactics were stereotyped by the national organizations of the various peoples. The true interest of the centuries of the early Middle Ages lies in the gradual evolution of new forms of warlike efficiency, which end in the establishment of a military class as the chief factor in war and the decay among most peoples of the old system which made the tribe arrayed in arms the normal fighting force. Intimately connected with this change was an alteration in arms and equipment, which transformed the outward appearance of war in a manner not less complete. This period of transition may be considered to end when, in the eleventh century, the feudal cavalier established his superiority over all the descriptions of troops which were pitted against him, from the Magyar horse archers of the east to the Anglo-Danish axmen of the west. The fight of Hastings, the last attempt made for three centuries by infantry to withstand cavalry, serves to mark the termination of the epoch.

The Teutonic tribes of northwestern Europe did not—like the Goths and Lombards—owe their victories to the strength of their mail-clad cavalry. The Franks and Saxons of the sixth and seventh centuries were still infantry. It would appear that the moors of northern Germany and Schleswig, and the heaths and marshes of Belgium, were less favorable to the growth of cavalry than were the steppes of the Ukraine or the plains of the Danube Valley.

The Frank, as pictured to us by Sidonius Apollinaris, Procopius, and Agathias, still bore a considerable resemblance to his Sicambrian ancestors. Like them he was destitute of helmet and body armor; his shield, however, had become a much more effective defense than the wicker framework of the first century: it was a solid oval with a large iron boss and rim. The framea had now been superseded by the *angon*—"a dart neither very long nor very short, which can be used against the enemy either by grasping it as a pike or hurling it." [1] The iron of its head extended far down the shaft; at its neck were two barbs, which made its extraction from a wound or a pierced shield almost impossible. The francisca, however, was the great weapon of the people from whom it derived its name. It was a single-bladed battle-ax,[2] with a heavy head composed of a long blade curved on its outer face and deeply hollowed in the interior. It was carefully weighted, so that it could be used, like an American tomahawk, for hurling at the enemy. The skill with which the Franks discharged this weapon, just before closing with the hostile line, was extraordinary, and its effectiveness made it their favorite arm. A sword and dagger (scramasax) completed the normal equipment of the warrior; the last was a broad thrusting blade 18 inches long, the former a two-edged cutting weapon about 2½ feet in length.

Such was the equipment of the armies which Theudebert, Buccelin, and Lothair led down into Italy in the middle of the sixth century. Procopius informs us that the first-named

---

[1] Agathias, *Historiarum libri quinque,* in *Corpus Scriptorum Historiae Byzantinae* (Bonn, 1828), I, 74.

[2] Though often called *bipennis,* it had not necessarily two blades, that word having become a mere general name for "ax."

prince brought with him some cavalry; their numbers, however, were insignificant, a few hundreds in an army of 90,000 men.[3] They carried the lance and a small round buckler, and served as a bodyguard round the person of the king. Their presence, though pointing to a new military departure among the Franks, only serves to show the continued predominance of infantry in their armies.

A problem interesting to the historian was worked out when in A.D. 554 the footmen of Buccelin met the Roman army of Narses at the battle of Casilinum. The superiority of the tactics and armament of the imperial troops was made equally conspicuous. Formed in one deep column, the Franks advanced into the center of the semicircle in which Narses had ranged his men. The Roman infantry and the dismounted heavy cavalry of the Herule auxiliaries held them in play in front, while the horse archers closed in on their flanks and inflicted on them the same fate which had befallen the army of Crassus. Hardly a man of Buccelin's followers escaped from the field. The day of infantry was gone, for the Franks as much as for the rest of the world.

We are accordingly not surprised to find that from the sixth to the ninth century a steady increase in the proportion of cavalry in the Frank armies is to be found; corresponding to it is an increased employment of defensive arms. A crested helmet of classical shape becomes common among them, and shortly after, a mail-shirt reaching to the hips is introduced. The emperor Charles the Great himself contributed to the armament of his cavalry by adopting defenses for the arms and thighs: *coxarum exteriora in eo*

[3] The 90,000 is certainly a gross exaggeration. See Lot, *op. cit.*, I, 41, 77.

ferreis ambiebantur bracteolis.[4] This protection, however, was at first rejected by many of the Franks, who complained that it impaired their seat on horseback.

[At Tours (A.D. 732), although a large part of the Frankish host may have ridden to battle, the tactics were purely those of the infantry square acting on the defensive. Even the withdrawal of the Saracens under cover of darkness did not provoke a Frankish pursuit. In the time of Charles the Great we are told that all men of importance, with their immediate followers, were accustomed to serve on horseback, and by the end of his reign, a very large proportion of the Frankish levy must have consisted of mounted men, while the infantry became less and less important. Charles also attempted to provide for a better armed host than had formerly attended the summons. The *Capitularies* are explicit in declaring that the local commanders "are to be careful that the men whom they have to lead to battle are fully equipped: that is, that they possess spear, shield, helm, mail-shirt (*brunia*), a bow, two bowstrings, and twelve arrows."[5] The Franks had therefore in the opening years of the ninth century begun to abandon their tradition of fighting exclusively on foot, and to entrust all important operations to their cavalry.

[This process may be regarded as complete when Charles the Bald decreed that *ut pagenses Franci qui caballos habent, aut habere possunt, cum suis comitibus in hostem pergant.*[6] Whether merely ratifying an existing state of things or instituting a new one, this order is significantly

[4] John Hewitt, *Ancient Armour and Weapons in Europe* (Oxford, 1855–1860), I, 8.

[5] *Capitularia regum Francorum*, ed. Alfred Boretius, in *Monumenta Germaniae Historica* (Hanover, 1833–1847), I, 171.

[6] *Capitularia*, II, 321.

characteristic of a period in which the defense of the country had fallen into the hands of its cavalry force alone. Of the causes which led to this consummation the most important was the character of the enemies with whom the Franks had to contend in the ninth and tenth centuries. The Northman in the western kingdom and the Magyar in the eastern were marauders bent on plunder alone, and owed their success to the rapidity of their movements. The hosts of the Vikings were in the habit of seizing horses in the country which they invaded, and then riding up and down the length of the land, always distancing the slowly moving local levies. The Hungarian horse archers conducted forays into the heart of Germany, yet succeeded in evading pursuit. For the repression of such inroads, infantry was absolutely useless; like the Romans of the fourth century, the Franks, when obliged to stand upon the defensive, had to rely upon their cavalry.

[This crisis in the military history of Europe coincided with the breaking up of all central power in the shipwreck of the dynasty of Charles the Great. In the absence of any centrally organized resistance, the defense of the empire fell into the hands of the local counts, who now became semi-independent sovereigns. To these petty rulers the landholders of each district now "commended" themselves, in order to obtain protection in an age of war and anarchy. At the same time, and for the same reason, the poorer freemen were "commending" themselves to the landholders. Thus the feudal hierarchy was established, and a new military system appeared, when the count or duke led out to battle his vassals and their mounted retainers.]

Politically retrogressive as was that system, it had yet its day of success: the Magyar was crushed at Riade near

Merseburg (A.D. 933) and the Lechfeld (A.D. 955) and driven back across the Leitha, soon to become Christianized and to grow into an orderly member of the European commonwealth. The Viking was checked in his plundering forays, expelled from his strongholds at the river mouths, and restricted to the single possession of Normandy, where he—like the Magyar—was assimilated to the rest of feudal society. The force which had won these victories and saved Europe from a relapse into the savagery and paganism of the north and east was that of the mailclad horseman. What wonder then if his contemporaries and successors glorified him into the normal type of warriorhood, and believed that no other form of military efficiency was worth cultivating? The perpetuation of feudal chivalry for four hundred years was the reward of its triumphs in the end of the Dark Ages.

Beyond the English Channel the course of the history of war is parallel to that which it took in the lands of the continent, with a single exception in the form of its final development. Like the Franks, the Angles and Saxons were at the time of their conquest of Britain a nation of infantry soldiers, armed with the long ashen javelin, the broadsword, the seax or broad stabbing dagger, and occasionally the battle-ax.[7] Their defensive weapon was almost exclusively the shield, the "round warboard," with its large iron boss. Ring mail, though known to them at a very early date, was, as all indications unite to show, extremely uncommon. The "grey war-sark" or "ring-locked byrnie" of Beowulf was obtainable by kings and princes alone. The helmet also, with its "iron-wrought boar-crest," was very restricted in

[7] A short weapon like the francisca, not the long Danish ax which afterwards became the national arm.

its use. If the monarch and his gesiths wore such arms, the national levy, which formed the main fighting force of a heptarchic kingdom, was entirely without them.

Unmolested for many centuries in their island home, the English kept up the old Teutonic war customs for a longer period than other European nations. When Mercia and Wessex were at strife, the campaign was fought out by the hastily raised hosts of the various districts, headed by their aldermen and reeves. Hence war bore the spasmodic and inconsequent character which resulted from the temporary nature of such armies. With so weak a military organization, there was no possibility of working out schemes of steady and progressive conquest. The frays of the various kingdoms, bitter and unceasing though they might be, led to no decisive results. If in the ninth century a tendency toward unification began to show itself in England, it was caused, not by the military superiority of Wessex, but by the dying out of royal lines and the unfortunate internal condition of the other states.

While this inclination toward union was developing itself, the whole island was subjected to the stress of the same storm of foreign invasion which was shaking the Frankish empire to its foundations. The Danes came down upon England and demonstrated, by the fearful success of their raids, that the old Teutonic military system was inadequate to the needs of the day. The Vikings were in fact superior to the forces brought against them, alike in tactics, in armament, in training, and in mobility. Personally the Dane was the member of an old war band contending with a farmer fresh from the plough, a veteran soldier pitted against a raw militiaman. As a professional warrior he had provided himself with an equipment which only the chiefs among the English army could rival, the mail byrnie being a normal rather than an exceptional defense, and the steel cap almost universal. The fyrd, on the other hand, came out against him destitute of armor, and bearing a motley array of weapons wherein the spear and sword were mixed with the club and the stone ax.[8] If, however, the Danes had been in the habit of waiting for the local levies to come up with them, equal courage and superior numbers might have prevailed over these advantages of equipment. Plunder, however, rather than fighting, was the Viking's object; the host threw itself upon some district of the English coast, "was there a-horsed," [9] and then rode far and wide through the land, doing all the damage in its power. The possession of the horses they had seized gave them a power of rapid movement which the fyrd could not hope to equal: when the local levies arrived at the spot where the invaders had been last seen, it was only to find smoke and ruins, not an enemy. When driven to bay—as, in spite of their habitual retreats, was sometimes the case—the Danes showed an instinctive tactical ability by their use of entrenchments, with which the English were unaccustomed to deal. Behind a ditch and palisade, in some commanding spot, the invaders would wait for months, till the accumulated force of the fyrd had melted away to its homes.

Of assaults on their positions they knew no fear, for the line of axmen could generally contrive to keep down the most impetuous charge of the English levies. Reading (A.D. 871) was a more typical field than Edington (A.D.

[8] If these were the *lignis imposita saxa* of which the Norman chronicler of Hastings spoke as being English weapons.

[9] *The Anglo-Saxon Chronicle*, ed. Benjamin Thorpe (Rolls Series; London, 1861), I, 130 and II, 59.

878). For one successful storm of an entrenched camp there were two bloody repulses.

[Though the Viking onslaught produced modifications in the existing system, which seemed to follow Frankish developments in some respects, the new military organization in England continued to rest solidly on the heavy armed infantryman as the individual unit.[10] While a feudal society did not evolve, there was a tendency toward the stratification of society, and under the pressure of constant warfare the more important freeholders were absorbed into the thegnly class, while the lesser ones sank into serfdom. The laws of Alfred indicate that the free middle class had become much less important than it had been in Ine's day. The thegn, who had originally been merely the sworn comrade of the king or war leader, now became a landed magnate, and although his position as such seems to have carried no legal obligation to furnish military service, he became *de facto* a military tenant. By the eleventh century there is no doubt but that a king's thegn, when summoned to military duty, must comply or suffer penalties which might include the confiscation of his land.[11] All holders of five hides and upwards were theoretically absorbed into the thegnhood, so that it was not a closed caste, but the military obligation seems to have been purely personal, and was not due from the land. The fyrd was retained, and continued to be the true national levy down to the fateful day of Hastings. In Alfred's time it was divided into two halves, one

[10] This paragraph and the four which follow have been completely rewritten by the editor to incorporate more recent findings. It is based in part on C. W. C. Oman, *A History of the Art of War in the Middle Ages* (London, 1924), I, 109–110.

[11] Frank M. Stenton, *The First Century of English Feudalism* (Ford Lectures; Oxford, 1932), pp. 114–119.

of which was available for active service while the other pursued its normal activities in the fields. This English force, based on the heavily armed foot soldier, was enabled to meet the Danes on an equal footing and to force a long period of armed truce. The settlement of the invaders in the Danelaw, moreover, greatly simplified the military problem of the English. An enemy with towns to be burned and fields to be ravaged was much more vulnerable than one whose base of operation was the open sea. It is noteworthy that Alfred, Edward the Elder, and his redoubtable sister, "the Lady of the Mercians," utilized a system of fortified posts or burhs, with stockades atop their earthen banks which held in check the raiders of the jarls of the Five Towns while the king and his forces were busy elsewhere.

[Within a century after the death of Alfred, the system again was subject to the test of an invasion. This time no strong leader emerged, and the forces of the local ealdormen were defeated in detail, with no attempt at anything like mutual support. The realm of Ethelred II was in an advanced stage of decentralization, with ealdormanries passing from father to son like the countships of Carolingian Francia. The strong administration of Cnut halted this process and at the same time introduced a new military element into the English scene: the standing body of household troops or housecarls. By 1066, not only the king but other great lords maintained such retainers, and many of them possessed considerable estates.[12] These professional soldiers represented the maximum of military efficiency to be found in the Anglo-Danish world.

[The tactics and weapons of the housecarls differed entirely from those of the feudal aristocracy of the continent

[12] *Ibid.*, pp. 119–120.

against whom they would be tested at Hastings. They were armed with the long Danish battle-ax, a shaft five feet long fitted with a single-bladed head of enormous size. It was far too ponderous for use on horseback and, being wielded with both arms, precluded the use of the shield in hand-to-hand combat. The blows delivered by this weapon were tremendous. No shield or mail could resist them; they were even capable, as was shown at Hastings, of lopping off a horse's head at a single stroke. The housecarl in his defensive equipment did not differ from the cavalry of the lands beyond the Channel: like them he wore a mail-shirt of a considerable length, reaching down to the lower thigh, and a pointed steel cap fitted with a nasal. The tactics of the English axmen were the normal infantry formations of column and line; arranged in a compact mass, they could beat off almost any attack and hew their way through every obstacle. Their personal strength and steadiness, their confidence, and their *esprit de corps* made them most dangerous adversaries. Their array, however, was vitiated by the two defects of slowness of movement and vulnerability to missiles. If assailed by horsemen, they were obliged to halt and remain fixed to the spot in order to keep off the enemy by their close order. If attacked from a distance by light troops, they were also at a disadvantage, as they were unable to reach men who retired before them.

[The battle of Hastings (October 14, 1066) was the last great mediaeval trial of arms in which infantry alone was pitted against feudal cavalry, until the thirteenth century was almost spent. King Harold, recently victorious over the Norwegians and his rebel brother Tostig at Stamford Bridge in Yorkshire, had hurried south upon learning of the Norman landing in Sussex. Rather than wait for the whole strength of the kingdom to assemble in arms, he, accompanied only by the housecarls of his own establishment and the hastily mobilized fyrd of the southern counties, threw himself between William and London. On the night of October 13, 1066, the Saxon army occupied the ridge at Senlac, eight miles north of Hastings, a strong defensive position where the London road debouched from the forest of the Weald. The authorities do not permit us to reconstruct the Saxon order of battle or to estimate its numerical strength. But on a front of some 1,100 yards, some 10,000 men may have been deployed,[13] where the dense mass of the Saxons might have stood firm forever against the assaults of the Norman cavalry.

[William had drawn up his host in three parallel corps, each composed of both infantry and cavalry. Each of the three divisions contained three lines: bowmen, heavily armed infantry, and the mailed horsemen, in that order. The fight was opened by the archers as the Norman host advanced to the attack. To this discharge the defenders were unable to reply until the first line came within javelin range, when it was driven back. The heavily armed foot soldiers, too, were unable to make the least impression on the shield wall of the Saxons. Finally Duke William launched his horsemen at the Saxon line, and after a furious collision it also withdrew discomfited. In fact, the withdrawal of the duke's left wing, composed chiefly of Bretons and Angevins, resembled a rout. Heartened by this success, a great mass of the English right broke from its position in pursuit of the flying Bretons. Seeing this, William wheeled

[13] This is Oman's latest estimate, *Art of War*, 2d ed., I, 156. Delbrück, in his *Geschichte* . . . , III, 153, would lower this figure to 4,000–7,000 on each side.

his center and took the pursuers in the flank, and in a brief time the ill-armed shire levies were cut to pieces. The great bulk of the Saxon host continued to stand on the defensive, and Duke William ordered another general assault, with little success. Then he resorted to the stratagem of a feigned flight by part of his army, and again a large group of Saxons broke ranks and followed the seemingly retreating Normans down the slope, where they were annihilated when the pursued turned to attack them head on. But the solid core of Harold's army, composed of the household troops, stood firmly along the crest of the ridge, and repeated cavalry assaults failed to shake them. Finally William ordered successive charges by the mailed horsemen, followed by volleys of arrows. This soon inflicted fearful casualties on the Saxons, who now could be taken in both front and flank. Nevertheless, the thinning ranks continued to hold the ridge throughout the day, and at dusk King Harold's banners, the Dragon of Wessex and the Fighting Man, still stood surrounded by the grimly fighting housecarls. It was the archer rather than the knight who settled the day, for a chance arrow pierced the eye of the heroic Harold, and a last charge of the Norman horse burst in among his dispirited followers, who fled into the forest at their rear. The tactics of the heavy armed foot soldier had been decisively beaten by Duke William's combination of archers and cavalry.]

Once more only—on a field far away from its native land —did the weapon of the Anglo-Danes dispute the victory with the lance and bow. Fifteen years after Harold's defeat another body of English axmen—some of them may well have fought at Hastings—were advancing against the army of a Norman prince. They were the Varangian guard, the

famous Πελεκυφόροι, of the emperor Alexius Comnenus.
That prince was engaged in an attempt to raise the siege of
Dyrrhachium (A.D. 1081) then invested by Robert Guis-
card. The Norman army was already drawn up in front of
its lines, while the troops of Alexius were only slowly ar-
riving on the field. Among the foremost of his corps were
the Varangians, whom his care had provided with horses
in order that they might get to the front quickly and execute a turning movement. This they accomplished, but
when they approached the enemy they were carried away
by their eagerness to begin the fray. Without waiting for
the main attack of the Greek army to be developed, the
axmen sent their horses to the rear and advanced in a solid
column against the Norman flank. Rushing upon the division commanded by Count Amaury of Bari, they drove
it, horse and foot, into the sea. Their success, however, had
disordered their ranks, and the Norman prince was enabled,
since Alexius' main body was still far distant, to turn all his
forces against them. A vigorous cavalry charge cut off the
greater part of the English; the remainder collected on a
little mound by the seashore, surmounted by a deserted
chapel. Here they were surrounded by the Normans, and a
scene much like Hastings, but on a smaller scale, was en-
acted. After the horsemen and the archers had destroyed
the majority of the Varangians, the remainder held out
obstinately within the chapel. Sending for fascines and
timber from his camp, Robert heaped them round the
building and set fire to the mass.[14] The English sallied out
to be slain one by one, or perished in the flames. Not a

[14] For these details see Anna Comnena, *The Alexiad*, tr. Elizabeth
Dawes (London, 1928), pp. 108–109. She calls the commander of
the Varangians Nabites. What English or Scandinavian name can

man escaped; the whole corps suffered destruction, as a consequence of their misplaced eagerness to open the fight. Such was the fate of the last attempt made by infantry to face the feudal array of the eleventh century. No similar experiment was now to be made for more than 200 years; the supremacy of cavalry was finally established.

---

this represent? Considering the remote resemblance of some of Anna Comnena's western names to their real forms, it is perhaps hopeless to expect an answer.

CHAPTER III

The Byzantines and
Their Enemies[1]

A.D. 582-1071

FROM THE ACCESSION OF MAURICE
TO THE BATTLE OF MANZIKERT

Character of Byzantine Strategy

ALIKE in composition and in organization, the army which
for 500 years held back Slav and Saracen from the frontier
of the eastern empire differed from the troops whose name
and traditions it inherited. To the Palatine and limitary
numeri of Constantine it bore as little likeness as to the
legions of Trajan. Yet in one respect at least it resembled
both those forces: it was in its day the most efficient military
body in the world. The men of the lower empire have received scant justice at the hands of modern historians; their
manifest faults have thrown the stronger points of their

---

[1] See especially: Maurice, *Artis militaris*, written about 595 A.D.;
Nicephorus II Phocas, νερι ναραδρομησ νολεμοτ, written about 960,
in *Corpus Scriptorum Historiae Byzantinae*, V (Bonn, 1828); and
Leo VI, the Wise, *Tactica*, written about 900 A.D., in Migne,
Patrologia Graeca, CVII (Paris, 1863).

character into the shade, and Byzantinism is accepted as a synonym for effete incapacity alike in peace and in war. Much might be written in general vindication of their age, but never is it easier to produce a strong defense than when their military skill and prowess are disparaged.

"The vices of Byzantine armies," says Gibbon, "were inherent, their victories accidental." So far is this sweeping condemnation from the truth that it would be far more correct to call their defeats accidental, their successes normal. Bad generalship, insufficient numbers, and unforeseen calamities, not the inefficiency of the troops, were the usual causes of disaster in the campaigns of the eastern emperors. To the excellence of the soldiery witness, direct or indirect, is borne in every one of those military treatises which give us such a vivid picture of the warfare of the age. Unless the general is incompetent or the surrounding circumstances are unusually adverse, the authors always assume that victory will follow the banner of the empire. The troops can be trusted, like Wellington's Peninsular veterans, "to go anywhere and do anything." "The commander," says Nicephorus Phocas,[2] "who has 6,000 of our heavy cavalry and God's help, needs nothing more." In a similar spirit Leo the Philosopher declares in his *Tactica* that, except for the Frankish and Lombard knights, there were no horsemen in the world who could face the Byzantine *cataphracti* when the numbers of the combatants approached equality. Slav, Turk, or Saracen could be ridden down by a charge fairly pressed home; only with the men of the West was the result of the shock doubtful. The causes of the excellence and efficiency of the Byzantine army are not hard to discover. In courage they were equal to their enemies; in discipline,

[2] Nicephorus II Phocas, *op. cit.*, p. 230.

organization, and armament, far superior. Above all, they possessed not only the traditions of Roman strategy but a complete system of tactics, carefully elaborated to suit the requirements of the age.

For centuries war was studied as an art in the east, while in the west it remained merely a matter of hard fighting. The young Frankish noble deemed his military education complete when he could sit his charger firmly and handle lance and shield with skill. The Byzantine patrician, while no less practiced in arms,[3] added theory to empiric knowledge by the study of the works of Maurice, of Leo, of Nicephorus Phocas, and of other authors whose books survive in name alone. The results of the opposite views taken by the two divisions of Europe are what might have been expected. The men of the west, though they regarded war as the most important occupation of life, invariably found themselves at a loss when opposed by an enemy with whose tactics they were not acquainted. The generals of the east, on the other hand, made it their boast that they knew how to face and conquer Slav or Turk, Frank or Saracen, by employing in each case the tactical means best adapted to meet their opponents' method of warfare.

The directions for the various emergencies given by the emperor Leo impress us alike as showing the diversity of the tasks set before the Byzantine general and the practical manner in which they were taken in hand. They serve indeed as a key to the whole system of the art of war as it was understood at Constantinople. According to Leo,

[3] Nothing better attests the military spirit of the eastern aristocracy than their duels; cf. the cases of Bardas Skleros and Bardas Phocas, in George Finlay, *History of the Byzantine Empire* (London, n.d.), pp. 335–339.

The Frank believes that a retreat under any circumstances must be dishonorable; hence he will fight whenever you choose to offer him battle. This you must not do until you have secured all possible advantages for yourself, as his cavalry, with their long lances and large shields, charge with a tremendous impetus. You should deal with him by protracting the campaign, and if possible lead him into the hills, where his cavalry are less efficient than in the plain. After a few weeks without a great battle his troops, who are very susceptible to fatigue and weariness, will grow tired of the war, and ride home in great numbers. . . . You will find him utterly careless as to outposts and reconnaissances, so that you can easily cut off outlying parties of his men, and attack his camp at advantage. As his forces have no bonds of discipline, but only those of kindred or oath, they fall into confusion after delivering their charge; you can therefore simulate flight, and then turn them, when you will find them in utter disarray. On the whole, however, it is easier and less costly to wear out a Frankish army by skirmishes and protracted operations rather than to attempt to destroy it at a single blow.[4]

The chapters of which these directions are an abstract have two distinct points of interest. They present us with a picture of a western army of the ninth or tenth century, the exact period of the development of feudal cavalry, drawn by the critical hand of an enemy. They also show the characteristic strength and weakness of Byzantine military science. On the one hand, we note that Leo's precepts are practical and efficacious; on the other, we see that they are based upon the supposition that the imperial troops

[4] Leo, *op. cit.*, ch. 18, cols. 966–967. The paragraphs here are a condensation of Leo's advice, and sometimes an elucidation, not a literal translation.

will normally act upon the defensive, a limitation which must materially lessen their efficiency. These, however, were the tactics by which the eastern emperors succeeded in maintaining their Italian themes for 400 years against every attack of Lombard duke or Frankish emperor.

The method which is recommended by Leo for resisting the "Turks" (by which name he denotes the Magyars and the tribes dwelling north of the Euxine) is different in every respect from that directed against the nations of the west. The Turkish army consisted of innumerable bands of light horsemen, who carried javelin and scimitar, but relied on their arrows for victory. Their tactics were in fact a repetition of those of Attila, a foreshadowing of those of Alp Arslan or Batu Khan. The Turks were "given to ambushes and stratagems of every sort," and were noted for the care with which they posted their vedettes, so that they could seldom or never be attacked by surprise. On a fair, open field, however, they could be ridden down by the Byzantine heavy cavalry, who are therefore recommended to close with them at once, and not to exchange arrows with them at a distance. Steady infantry they could not break, and indeed they were averse to attacking it, since the bows of the Byzantine foot archers carried farther than their own shorter weapon and they were thus liable to have their horses shot before coming within their own limit of efficacious range. Their armor protected their own bodies, but not those of their chargers; and they might thus find themselves dismounted, in which position they were absolutely helpless, the nomad of the steppes never having been accustomed to fight on foot. With the Turks, therefore, a pitched battle was desirable; but as they were prompt at rallying, it was always necessary to pursue them with caution, and not to allow the troops to get out of hand during the chase.

It is at once apparent from these directions how utterly the efficiency of the Byzantine infantry differed from that of the legions of an earlier day. The soldiers of the first century, armed with sword and pilum alone, were destroyed from a distance by the Parthian mounted bowmen. The adoption of the bow by infantry had now changed the aspect of affairs, and it was the horse archer who now found himself at a disadvantage in the exchange of missiles. Nor could he hope to retrieve the day by charging, since the *scutati*,[5] or spearmen carrying the large shield, who formed the front rank of a Byzantine *tagma*, could keep at bay horsemen armed, not with the heavy lance of the west, but merely with scimitars and short javelins. Hence the Turk avoided conflicts with the imperial infantry and used his superior powers of locomotion to keep out of its way. It was only the cavalry which could, as a rule, come up with him.

The tactics calculated for success against the Slavs call for little notice. The Serbians and the Slovenes possessed hardly any cavalry, and were chiefly formidable to the imperial troops when they kept to the mountains, where their archers and javelin men, posted in inaccessible positions, could annoy the invader from a distance or the spearmen could make sudden assaults on the flank of his marching columns. Such attacks could be frustrated by proper vigilance, while, if the Slavs were only surprised while en-

[5] σκουτάτοι, one of the curious Latin survivals in Byzantine military terminology. In transliterating Latin words the Greeks paid no attention to quantity.

gaged in their plundering expeditions into the plains, they could be ridden down and cut to pieces by the imperial cavalry.

To deal with the Saracen,[6] on the other hand, the greatest care and skill were required. "Of all barbarous nations," says Leo, "they are the best advised and the most prudent in their military operations."[7] The commander who has to meet with them will need all his tactical and strategical ability, the troops must be well disciplined and confident, if the "barbarous and blaspheming Saracen"[8] is to be driven back in rout through the passes of the Taurus.

The Arabs whom Khaled and Amru had led in the seventh century to the conquest of Syria and Egypt had owed their victory neither to the superiority of their arms nor to the excellence of their organization. The fanatical courage of the fatalist had enabled them to face better-armed and better-disciplined troops. Settled in their new homes, however, when the first outburst of their vigor had passed away, they did not disdain to learn a lesson from the nations they had defeated. Accordingly the Byzantine army served as a model for the forces of the Caliphs. "They have copied the Romans in most of their military practices," says Leo,[9] "both in arms and in strategy. Like the imperial generals, they placed their confidence in their mailed lancers; but the Saracen and his charger were alike at a disadvantage in the onset. Horse for horse and man for man, the Byzantines

[6] Much confusion in military history has been caused by writers attributing the archery of the Turks to the Saracens; the latter were not employers of archery tactics, but lancers. Battles like Dorylaeum, which are given as examples of Saracen warfare, were fought really by Turks.

[7] Leo, *op. cit.*, ch. 18, col. 975. .   [8] *Ibid.*

[9] *Ibid.*, col. 974.

were heavier, and could ride the Orientals down when the final shock came."

Two things alone rendered the Saracens the most dangerous of foes: their numbers and their extraordinary powers of locomotion. When an inroad into Asia Minor was projected, the powers of greed and fanaticism united to draw together every unquiet spirit between Khorasan and Egypt. The wild horsemen of the east poured out in myriads from the gates of Tarsus and Adana, to harry the fertile uplands of the Anatolic themes.

They are no regular troops, but a mixed multitude of volunteers: the rich man serves from pride of race, the poor man from hope of plunder. Many of them go forth because they believe that God delights in war, and has promised victory to them. Those who stay at home, both men and women, aid in arming their poorer neighbours, and think that they are performing a good work thereby. Thus there is no homogeneity in their armies, since experienced warriors and untrained plunderers march side by side.[10]

Once clear of the passes of Taurus, the great horde of Saracen horsemen cut itself loose from its communications and rode far and wide through Phrygia and Cappadocia, burning the open towns, harrying the countryside, and lading their beasts of burden with the plunder of a region which was in those days one of the richest in the world.

Now was the time for the Byzantine general to show his mettle: first he had to come up with his enemies, and then to fight them. The former task was no easy matter, as the Saracen in the first days of his inroad could cover an incredi-

[10] *Ibid.*, various scattered notices in ch. 18, cols. 946–990.

ble distance. It was not till he had loaded and clogged himself with plunder that he was usually to be caught.

When the news of the raid reached the general of the Anatolic or Armeniac theme, he had at once to collect every efficient horseman in his province and strike at the enemy. Untrained men and weak horses were left behind, and the infantry could not hope to keep up with the rapid movements which had now to be undertaken. Accordingly, Leo would send all the disposable foot to occupy the passes of the Taurus, where, even if the cavalry did not catch the invader, his retreat might be delayed and harassed in passes where he could not fight to advantage.

In his cavalry, however, lay the Byzantine commander's hope of success. To ascertain the enemy's position he must spare no trouble: "Never turn away freeman or slave, by day or night, though you may be sleeping or eating or bathing," writes Nicephorus Phocas, "if he says that he has news for you." When once the Saracen's track had been discovered, he was to be pursued without ceasing, and his force and objects discovered. If all Syria and Mesopotamia had come out for an invasion rather than a mere foray, the general must resign himself to taking the defensive, and only hang on the enemy's flanks, cutting off his stragglers and preventing any plundering by detached parties. No fighting must be taken in hand till "all the themes of the east have been set marching;" an order which would put some 25,000 or 30,000 heavy cavalry [11] at the disposal of

[11] In Leo's day the Oriental themes had not been subdivided, as was afterwards done by his son Constantine. There were then eight themes in Asia Minor, each of which contained a military division of the same name and could be reckoned on for some 4,000 heavy

the commander-in-chief but would cause the loss of much precious time. These Saracen raids in force were of comparatively infrequent occurrence; it was seldom that the whole Byzantine force in Asia was drawn out to face the enemy in a great battle. The more typical Saracen inroad was made by the inhabitants of Cilicia and northern Syria, with the assistance of casual adventurers from the inner Mohammedan lands.

To meet them the Byzantine commander would probably have no more than the 4,000 heavy cavalry of his own theme in hand, a force for whose handling Leo gives minute tactical directions.[12] When he had come up with the raiders they would turn and offer him battle, nor was their onset to be despised. Though unequal, man for man, to their adversaries, they were usually in superior numbers, and always came on with great confidence. "They are very bold at first with expectation of victory; nor will they turn at once, even if their line is broken through by our impact." [13] When they suppose that their enemy's vigor is relaxing, they all charge together with a desperate effort.[14] If, however, this fails, a rout generally ensues, "for they think that all misfortune is sent by God, and so, if they are once beaten, they take their defeat as a sign of divine wrath, and

cavalry. These were "Armeniacon, Anatolicon, Obsequium, Thracesion, Cibyrrhoeot, Bucellarion, and Paphlagonian." Optimaton, the ninth theme, had (as Constantine tells us in his treatise on the empire) no military establishments. Professor Oman maintained this interpretation of Leo in the final edition of his work, I, 211–212. But Lot, *op. cit.*, I, 66–68, believes that there is sufficient reason to doubt that the eastern Roman empire could put 30,000 heavy cavalry in the field in the ninth century.

[12] See the next section of this treatise for the plan of his formation, p. 52.

[13] *Tactica*, ch. 18, col. 974.   [14] *Ibid.*, col. 979.

no longer attempt to defend themselves." [15] Hence the Mussulman army, when once it turned to fly, could be pursued *à l'outrance,* and the old military maxim *Vince sed ne nimis vincas* was a caution which the Byzantine officer could disregard.

The secret of success in an engagement with the Saracens lay in the cavalry tactics, which had for three centuries been in process of elaboration. By the tenth century they attained their perfection, and the experienced soldier Nicephorus Phocas vouches for their efficacy. Their distinguishing feature was that the troops were always placed in two lines and a reserve, with squadrons detached on the flanks to prevent their being turned. The enemy came on in one very deep line, and could never stand the three successive shocks as the first line, second line, and reserve were one after another flung into the melee against them. The Byzantines had already discovered the great precept that, in a cavalry combat, the side which holds back the last reserve must win. The exact formation used on these occasions, carefully described by our authorities, is worth detailing, and will be found in the section treating of the organization of the Byzantine army.

There were several other methods of dealing with the Saracen invader. It was sometimes advisable, when his inroad was made in great force, to hang about the rear of the retreating plunderers, and only fall upon them when they were engaged in passing the defiles of the Taurus. If infantry was already on the spot to aid the pursuing cavalry, success was almost certain when the Saracens and their train of beasts, laden with spoil, were wedged in the passes. They could then be shot down by the archers, and would

[15] *Ibid.,* col. 974.

not stand for a moment when they saw their horses, "the *Pharii,* whom they esteem above all other things," [16] struck by arrows from a distance, for the Saracen, when not actually engaged in close combat, would do anything to save his horse from harm.

Cold and rainy weather was also distasteful to the Oriental invader; at times when it prevailed, he did not display his ordinary firmness and daring, and could be attacked to great advantage. Much could also be done by delivering a vigorous raid into his country and wasting Cilicia and northern Syria the moment his armies were reported to have passed north into Cappadocia. This destructive practice was very frequently adopted, and the sight of two armies each ravaging the other's territory without attempting to defend its own was only too familiar to the inhabitants of the borderlands of Christendom and Islam. Incursions by sea supplemented the forays by land. Leo says:

When the Saracens of Cilicia have gone off by the passes, to harry the country north of Taurus, the commander of the Cibyrrhoeot theme should immediately go on shipboard with all available forces, and ravage their coast. If, on the other hand, they have sailed off to attempt the shore districts of Pisidia, the Klissurarchs of Taurus can lay waste the territories of Tarsus and Adana without danger.[17]

Nothing can show more clearly than these directions the high average skill of the Byzantine officer. Leo himself was not a man of any great ability, and his *Tactica* is intended to codify an existing military art, rather than to construct a new one. Yet the book is one whose equal could not have

[16] *Ibid.,* cols. 978–979.   [17] *Ibid.,* col. 979.

been written in western Europe before the sixteenth century. One of its most striking points is the utter difference of its tone from that of contemporary feeling in the rest of Christendom. Of chivalry there is not a spark in the Byzantine, though professional pride is abundantly shown. Courage is regarded as one of the requisites necessary for obtaining success, not as the sole and paramount virtue of the warrior. Leo considers a campaign successfully concluded without a great battle as the cheapest and most satisfactory consummation in war. He has no respect for the warlike ardor which makes men eager to plunge into the fray: it is to him rather a characteristic of the ignorant barbarian, and an attribute fatal to anyone who makes any pretension to generalship.

He shows a strong predilection for stratagems, ambushes, and simulated retreats. For an officer who fights without having first secured all the advantages to his own side, he has the greatest contempt. It is with a kind of intellectual pride that he gives instructions how *parlementaires* are to be sent to the enemy without any real object except that of spying out the number and efficiency of his forces. He gives, as a piece of most ordinary and moral advice, the hint that a defeated general may often find time to execute a retreat by sending an emissary to propose a surrender (which he has no intention of carrying out) to the hostile commander. He is not above employing the old-world trick of addressing treasonable letters to the subordinate officers of the enemy's army, and contriving that they should fall into the hands of the commander-in-chief, in order that he may be made suspicious of his lieutenants. Schemes such as these are "Byzantine" in the worst sense of the word, but their character must not be allowed to blind us to the real

and extraordinary merits of the strategical system into
which they have been inserted. The art of war, as understood at Constantinople in the tenth century, was the only
scheme of true scientific merit existing in the world, and
was unrivaled till the sixteenth century.

Arms, Organization, and Tactics of the Byzantine Armies

The Byzantine army may be said to owe its peculiar
form to the emperor Maurice, a prince whose reign is one
of the chief landmarks in the history of the lower empire.[18]
The fortunate preservation of his *Artis militaris* suffices to
show us that the reorganization of the troops of the east
was mainly due to him. Contemporary historians also mention his reforms, but without descending to details, and
inform us that, though destined to endure, they won him
much unpopularity among the soldiery. Later writers, however, have erroneously attributed these changes to the
more celebrated warrior Heraclius,[19] the prince who bore
the Roman standards farther than any of his predecessors
into the lands of the East. In reality, the army of Heraclius
had already been reorganized by the worthy but unfortunate Maurice.

The most important of Maurice's alterations was the
elimination of that system somewhat resembling the Teutonic *comitatus,* which had crept from among the *foederati*

[18] The Middle Ages dimly felt this, and (as Gibbon tells us) the
Italian Chroniclers name him the "first of the Greek Emperors" (Ed-
ward Gibbon, *The Decline and Fall of the Roman Empire* [Modern
Library; New York, n.d.], II, 397).

[19] As, for example, the emperor Constantine Porphyrogenitus,
who, in his book on the *Themata Orientis,* attributes the invention of the "theme" and *tagma* to Heraclius.

into the ranks of the regular Roman army. The loyalty of
the soldier was secured rather to the emperor than to his
immediate superiors by making the appointment of all
officers above the rank of centurion a care of the central
government. The commander of an army or division had
thus no longer in his hands the power and patronage which
had given him the opportunity of becoming dangerous to
the state. The men found themselves under the orders of
delegates of the emperor, not of quasi-independent authorities who enlisted them as personal followers rather than as
units in the military establishment of the empire.

This reform Maurice succeeded in carrying out, to the
great benefit of the discipline and loyalty of his army. He
next took in hand the reducing of the whole force of the
empire to a single form of organization. The rapid decrease
of the revenues of the state, which had set in toward the
end of Justinian's reign and continued to make itself more
and more felt, had apparently resulted in a great diminu-
tion in the number of foreign mercenaries serving in the
Roman army. The same end was hastened by the fact that
of the nations who had furnished the majority of the imperial *foederati*, the Lombards had migrated to Italy, while
the Herules and Gepids had been exterminated. At last
the number of the foreign corps had sunk to such a low
ebb that there was no military danger incurred in assimilat-
ing their organization into that of the rest of the army.

The new system introduced by Maurice was destined
to last for nearly five hundred years. Its unit, alike for infantry and cavalry, was the βάνδον [20]—a weak battalion or

---

[20] Βάνδον, *bandum,* had become a common word in Justinian's
time; it is used as a Teutonic equivalent for *vexillum* in both its
senses.

horse regiment of 400 men, commanded by an officer who usually bore the vulgarized title of comes,[21] but was occasionally denominated by the older name of τριβῶνος, or military tribune. Three or more "bands" (or τάγματα, as they were sometimes styled) formed a small brigade, called variously μοῖρα, χιλιαρχία, or δροῦγγος.[22] Three *drunges* formed the largest military group recognized by Maurice, and the division made by their union was the turma or μέρος. Nothing can be more characteristic of the whole Byzantine military system than the curious juxtaposition of Latin, Greek, and German words in its terminology. Upon the substratum of the old Roman survivals we find first a layer of Teutonic names introduced by the *foederati* of the fourth and fifth centuries, and finally numerous Greek denominations, some of them borrowed from the old Macedonian military system, others newly invented. The whole official language of the empire was in fact still in a state of flux; Maurice himself was hailed by his subjects as Pius, Felix, Augustus,[23] though those who used the title were, for the most part, accustomed to speak in Greek. In the *Artis militaris* the two tongues are inextricably mixed: "Before the battle," says the emperor, "let the counts face their bands and raise the war-cry 'Δεοῦς Νοβισκοῦμ' (*Deus nobiscum*), and the troopers will shout the answering cry 'Κύριε, Ἐλέησον.'"

It would appear that Maurice had intended to break down the barrier which had been interposed in the fourth

[21] Comes had in Constantine's days been applied to five great officers alone.

[22] This curious word is first found in Vegetius, where it is only applied to the masses of a barbarian army. (Cf. English "throng.")

[23] See the evidence of coins: the title πιστός εν θεῳ βασιλευς των ρωμαιων only becomes common under the Amorian dynasty.

century between the class which paid the taxes and that which recruited the national army. "We wish," he writes, "that every young Roman of free condition should learn the use of the bow, and should be constantly provided with that weapon and with two javelins." If, however, this was intended to be the first step toward the introduction of universal military service, the design was never carried any further. Three hundred years later Leo is found echoing the same words, as a pious wish rather than as a practical expedient. The rank and file, however, of the imperial forces were now raised almost entirely within the realm, and well-nigh every nation contained in its limits, except the Greeks, furnished a considerable number of soldiers. The Armenians and Isaurians in Asia and the Thracians and Macedonians—or more properly the semi-Romanized Slavs —in Europe were considered the best material by the recruiting officer.

The extraordinary permanence of all Byzantine institutions is illustrated by the fact that Maurice's arrangements were found almost unchanged 300 years after his death. The chapters of Leo's *Tactica* which deal with the armament and organization of the troops are little more than a re-edition of the similar parts of his predecessor's *Artis militaris*. The descriptions of the heavy and light horseman and of the infantry soldier are identical in the two works except in a few points of terminology.

The καβαλλάριος, or heavy trooper, wore at both epochs a steel cap, surmounted by a small crest, and a long mail-shirt, reaching from the neck to the thighs. He was also protected by gauntlets and steel shoes, and usually wore a light surcoat over his mail. The horses of the officers and of the men in the front rank were furnished with steel

frontlets and poitrails. The arms of the soldier were a broadsword (σπάθιον), a dagger (παραμήριον), a horseman's bow
and quiver, and a long lance (κοντάριον), fitted with a
thong toward its butt and ornamented with a little bannerole. The color of bannerole, crest, and surcoat was that
of the regimental standard, and no two "bands" in the
same turma had standards of the same hue. Thus the line
presented a uniform and orderly appearance, every band
displaying its own regimental facings. Strapped to his sad-
dle each horseman carried a long cloak, which he assumed
in cold and rainy weather or when, for purposes of conceal-
ment, he wished to avoid displaying the glitter of his
armor.[24]

The light trooper had less complete equipment, sometimes a cuirass of mail or horn, at others only a light mail
cape covering the neck and shoulders. He carried a large
shield, a defense which the heavy horseman could not
adopt on account of his requiring both hands to draw his
bow. For arms the light cavalry carried lance and sword.

The infantry, which was much inferior to the horsemen
in importance, was, like them, divided into two descriptions, heavy and light. The *scutati* (σκουτάτοι), or troops of
the former class, wore a steel helmet with a crest, and a
short mail-shirt; they carried a large, oblong shield (θύρις),
which, like their crests, was of the same color as the regimental banner. Their chief weapon was a short but heavy
battle-ax (τζικούριον = *securis*) with a blade in front and
a spike behind; they were also provided with a dagger. The
light infantry (ψιλοί) wore no defensive armor; they were
provided with a powerful bow, which carried much farther
than the horseman's weapon and was therefore very formi-

[24] *Tactica*, ch. 12, cols. 806–843.

dable to hostile horse archers. A few corps, drawn from provinces where the bow was not well known, carried instead two or three javelins (ῥιπτάρια). For hand-to-hand fighting the *psiloi* were provided with an ax similar to that of the scutati and a very small, round target, which hung at their waists.[25]

An extensive train of noncombatants was attached to the army. Among the cavalry every four troopers had a groom; among the infantry every sixteen men were provided with an attendant, who drove a cart containing "a hand-mill, a bill-hook, a saw, two spades, a mallet, a large wicker basket, a scythe, and two pick-axes," [26] besides several other utensils for whose identity the dictionary gives no clue.[27] Thus twenty spades and twenty pickaxes per "century" [28] were always forthcoming for entrenching purposes. So perfect was the organization of the Byzantine army that it contained not only a "military train" but even an ambulance corps of bearers (σκριβῶνοι) and surgeons. The value attached to the lives of the soldiery is shown by the fact that the *scriboni* received a nomisma [29] for every wounded man whom they brought off when the troops were retiring. Special officers were told to superintend the march of this mass of noncombatants and vehicles, which is collectively styled *tuldum* (τοῦλδον), and forms not the least part among the cares of the laborious author of the *Tactica*.

Those portions of the works of Maurice and Leo which deal with tactics show a far greater difference between the

[25] *Ibid.*, ch. 6, cols. 722–734.   [26] *Ibid.*, col. 730.

[27] E.g., a κελίκον and a ματζούκιον.

[28] The century contained 10 decuries, but the decury was 16, not 10, men; thus the century was 160 strong. Three centuries went to a "band," which would thus be about 450 men.

[29] Gold coin, worth perhaps 12*s.* in metal value.

methods of the sixth and the ninth centuries than is observable in other parts of their military systems. The chapters of Leo are, as is but natural, of a more interesting character than are those of his predecessor. The more important of his ordinances are well worth our attention.

It is first observable that the old Roman system of drawing entrenchments round the army every time that it rested for the night had been resumed. A corps of engineers (Μένσορες [*sic*]) always marched with the vanguard and, when the evening halt had been called, traced out with stakes and ropes the contour of the camp. When the main body had come up, the *tuldum* was placed in the center of the enclosure, while the infantry "bands" drew a ditch and bank along the lines of the Mensores' ropes, each corps doing a fixed amount of the work. A thick chain of pickets was kept far out from the camp, so that a surprise, even on the darkest of nights, was almost impossible.[30]

The main characteristic of the Byzantine system of tactics is the small size of the various units employed in the operations, a sure sign of the existence of a high degree of discipline and training. While a western army went on its blundering way arranged in two or three enormous "battles," each mustering many thousand men, a Byzantine army of equal strength would be divided into many scores of fractions. Leo does not seem to contemplate the existence of any column of greater strength than that of a single "band." The fact that order and cohesion could be found in a line composed of so many separate units is the best testimony to the high average ability of the officers in

[30] Nicephorus Phocas in his Παραδρομη Πολεμου says that "Armenians must never be placed in this line of pickets as their habitual drowsiness at night makes them untrustworthy" (pp. 188–189).

subordinate commands. These counts and *moirarchs* were in the ninth and tenth centuries drawn for the most part from the ranks of the Byzantine aristocracy. Leo says:

Nothing prevents us from finding a sufficient supply of men of wealth, and also of courage and high birth, to officer our army. Their nobility makes them respected by the soldiers, while their wealth enables them to win the greatest popularity among their troops by the occasional and judicious gift of small creature-comforts.[31]

A true military spirit existed among the noble families of the eastern empire; houses like those of Skleros and Phocas, of Bryennius, Kerkuas, and Comnenus are found furnishing generation after generation of officers to the national army. The patrician left luxury and intrigue behind him when he passed through the gates of Constantinople, and became in the field a keen professional soldier.[32]

Infantry plays in Leo's work a very secondary part. So much is this the case that in many of his tactical directions he gives a sketch of the order to be observed by the cavalry alone, without mentioning the foot. This results from the fact that when the conflict was one with a rapidly moving foe like the Saracen or Turk, the infantry would at the moment of battle be in all probability many marches in the

[31] Leo, *op. cit.*, ch. 4, cols. 698–699.

[32] Nothing gives a better idea of the real military character of the Byzantine aristocracy than a perusal of the curious tenth-century romance of "Digenes Akritas," a member of the house of Ducas who is Klissurarch of the passes of Taurus and performs with his mighty mace all the exploits of a hero of chivalry. He really existed, and bore the name of Basil Pantherios (C. Diehl, "Byzantine Civilization," ch. xxiv in *Cambridge Mediaeval History* [London, 1936], IV, 76).

rear. It is, therefore, with the design of showing the most typical development of Byzantine tactics that a turma of nine "bands," or 3,500 to 4,000 men, as placed in order, be-

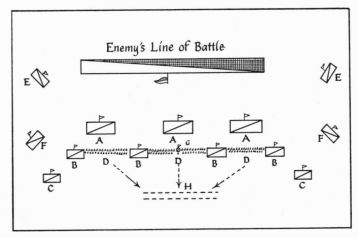

Fig. 1. A Byzantine cavalry turma in order of battle.

A.A.A.—front line, three *banda* of about 450 men each; B.B.B.B. —second line, four half-*banda* of about 225 men each; C.C.—reserve, two half-*banda* of same force; D.D.D.—one *bandon* in double rank filling the intervals of the second line; E.E.—ἔνεδροι, or detached bodies at the wings, who are to turn the enemy's flanks: 225 each or one *bandon* together; F.F.—πλαγιοσύλακες, troops posted to prevent similar attempts of the enemy: 225 each, or one *bandon* together; G.—commander and his staff; H.—place to which the troops D.D.D. would retire, when second line charged.

fore engaging with an enemy whose force consists of horsemen, has been selected for description.

The front line consisted of three *banda*, each drawn up in a line seven (or occasionally five) deep. These troops were to receive the first shock. Behind the first line was arranged a second, consisting of four half-*banda*, each drawn up ten (or occasionally eight) deep. They were placed not directly behind the front bands, but in the intervals between them, so that, if the first line was repulsed, they might fall back, not on to their comrades, but into the spaces between them. To produce, however, an impression of solidity in the second line, a single *bandon* was divided into three parts, and its men were drawn up, two deep, in the spaces between the four half-*banda*. These troops, on seeing the men of the first line beaten back and falling into the intervals of the second line, were directed to wheel to the rear and form a support behind the center of the array. The main reserve, however, consisted of two half-*banda*, posted on the flanks of the second line but considerably to the rear. It was in line with these that the retiring *bandon* would array itself. To each flank of the main body was attached a half-*bandon* of 225 men; these were called πλαγιοφύλακες and were entrusted with the duty of resisting attempts to turn the flanks of the turma. Still farther out, and if possible under cover, were placed two other bodies of similar strength; it was their duty to endeavor to get into the enemy's rear, or at any rate to disturb his wings by unexpected assaults; these troops were called ῎Ενεδροι, or "liers-in-wait." The commander's position was normally in the center of the second line, where he would be able to obtain a better general idea of the fight than if he at once threw himself into the melee at the head of the foremost squadrons.

This order of battle is deserving of all praise. It provided for that succession of shocks which is the key to victory in a cavalry combat; as many as five different attacks could be made on the enemy before all the impetus of the Byzantine force had been exhausted. The arrangement of the second line behind the intervals of the first obviated the possibility of the whole force being disordered by the repulse of the first squadrons. The routed troops would have behind them a clear space in which to rally, not a close line into which they would carry their disarray. Finally, the charge of the reserve and the detached troops would be made not on the enemy's center, which would be covered by the remains of the first and second lines, but on his flank, his most uncovered and vulnerable point.

A further idea of the excellent organization of the Byzantine army will be given by the fact that in minor engagements each corps was told off into two parts, one of which, the *cursores* (κούρσορες), represented the "skirmishing line" and the other, the *defensores* (διφένσορες), "the supports." The former in the case of the infantry turma would of course consist of the archers, the latter of the *scutati*.

To give a complete sketch of Leo's *Tactics* would be tedious and unnecessary. Enough indications have now been given to show their strength and completeness. It is easy to understand, after a perusal of such directions, the permanence of the military power of the eastern empire. Against the undisciplined Slav and Saracen the imperial troops had on all normal occasions the tremendous advantages of science and discipline. It is their defeats rather than their victories which need an explanation.

The termination of the period of Byzantine greatness was the battle of Manzikert, A.D. 1071. At this fight the rashness of Romanus Diogenes led to the annihilation of the forces of the Asiatic themes by the horse archers of Alp Arslan. The decay of the central power which was marked by the rise of Isaac Comnenus, the nominee of the feudal party of

Asiatic nobles, may have already enfeebled the army. It was, however, the result of Manzikert which was fatal to it, as the occupation of the themes of the interior of Asia Minor by the Seljuk Turks cut off from the empire its greatest recruiting ground, the land of the gallant Isaurians and Armenians, who had for five hundred years formed the core of the eastern army.

It will be observed that no long account of the famous Greek fire, the one point in Byzantine military affairs which most authors condescend to notice, has been given. This neglect is from a conviction that, although its importance in poliorcetics and naval fighting was considerable, it was, after all, a minor engine of war, and not comparable as a cause of Byzantine success to the excellent strategical and tactical system. Very much the same conclusion may be drawn from a study of the other purely mechanical devices which existed in the hands of the imperial generals. The old skill of the Roman engineer was preserved almost in its entirety, and the armories of Constantinople were filled with machines whose deadly efficacy inspired the ruder peoples of the west and east with a mysterious feeling of awe. The *vinea* and *testudo,* the catapult, onager and ballista, were as well known in the tenth century as in the first. They were undoubtedly employed, and employed with effect, at every siege. But no amount of technical skill in the use of military machines would have sufficed to account for the ascendancy enjoyed by the Byzantines over their warlike neighbors. The sources of that superiority are to be sought in the existence of science and discipline, of strategy and tactics, of a professional and yet national army, of an upper class at once educated and military. When the aristocracy became mere courtiers, when foreign mercenaries superseded the Isaurian bowman and the Anatolic cavalier, when the traditions of the old Roman organization gave place to mere centralization, then no amount of the inherited mechanical skill of past ages could save the Byzantine Empire from its fall. The rude vigor of the western knight accomplished the task which Chosroes and Crumn, Moslemah and Sviatoslav, had found too hard for them. But it was not the empire of Heraclius or John I Zimisces, of Leo III, the Isaurian, or Leo V, the Armenian, that was subdued by the piratical Crusaders; it was only the diminished and disorganized realm of the miserable Alexius III, Angelus.

CHAPTER IV

The Supremacy of
Feudal Cavalry

A.D. 1066-1346

FROM THE BATTLE OF HASTINGS TO THE
BATTLES OF MORGARTEN AND CRÉCY

BETWEEN the last struggles of the infantry of the Anglo-Dane and the rise of the pikemen and bowmen of the fourteenth century lies the period of the supremacy of the mail-clad feudal horseman. The epoch is, as far as strategy and tactics are concerned, one of almost complete stagnation; only in the single branch of poliorcetics does the art of war make any appreciable progress.

The feudal organization of society made every person of gentle blood a fighting man, but it cannot be said that it made him a soldier. If he could sit his charger steadily and handle lance and sword with skill, the horseman of the twelfth or thirteenth century was regarded as a model of military efficiency. That discipline or tactical skill may be as important to an army as mere courage he had no conception. Assembled with difficulty, insubordinate, unable to maneuver, ready to melt away from its standard the moment that its short period of service was over, a feudal force presented an assemblage of unsoldierlike qualities such as have seldom been known to coexist. Primarily intended to defend its own borders from the Magyar, the Northman, or the Saracen, the foes who in the tenth century had been a real danger to Christendom, the institution was utterly unadapted to take the offensive. When a number of tenants in chief had come together, each blindly jealous of his fellows and recognizing no superior but the king— and often even the king was powerless to control his nobles —it would require a leader of uncommon skill to persuade them to institute that hierarchy of command which must be established in every army that is to be something more than an undisciplined mob. Monarchs might try to obviate the danger by the creation of offices such as those of the constable and marshal, but these expedients were mere palliatives. The radical vice of insubordination continued to exist. It was always possible that at some critical moment a battle might be precipitated, a formation broken, a plan disconcerted, by the rashness of some petty baron or banneret who could listen to nothing but the promptings of his own heady valor. When the hierarchy of command was based on social status rather than on professional experience, the noble who led the largest contingent or held the highest rank felt himself entitled to assume the direction of the battle. The veteran who brought only a few lances to the array could seldom aspire to influencing the movements of his superiors.

When mere courage takes the place of skill and experience, tactics and strategy alike disappear. Arrogance and stupidity combined to give a certain definite color to the proceedings of the average feudal host. The century and the land may differ, but the incidents of battle are the same: El Mansûra (A.D. 1250) is like Aljubarrota (A.D. 1385); Nicopolis (A.D. 1396) is like Courtrai (A.D. 1302). When the enemy came into sight, nothing could restrain the western knights; the shield was shifted into position, the lance dropped into rest, the spur touched the charger, and the mailclad line thundered on, regardless of what might be before it. As often as not its career ended in being dashed against a stone wall or tumbled into a canal, in painful flounderings in a bog or futile surgings around a palisade. The enemy who possessed even a rudimentary system of tactics could hardly fail to be successful against such armies. The fight of El Mansûra (A.D. 1250) may be taken as a fair specimen of the military customs of the thirteenth century. When the French vanguard saw a fair field before them and the lances of the infidel gleaming among the palm groves, they could not restrain their eagerness. With the Count of Artois at their head, they started off in a head-long charge, in spite of St. Louis' [Louis IX] strict prohibition of an engagement. The Mamelukes retreated, allowed their pursuers to entangle themselves in the streets of a town, and then turned fiercely on them from all sides at once. In a short time the whole "battle" of the Count of Artois was dispersed and cut to pieces. Meanwhile the main body, hearing of the danger of their companions, had ridden off hastily to their aid. However, as each commander took his own route and made what speed he could, the French army arrived upon the field in dozens of small scattered bodies. These were attacked in detail, and in many cases routed by the Mamelukes. No general battle was fought, but a number of detached and incoherent cavalry combats had all the results of a great defeat. A skirmish and a street fight could overthrow the chivalry of the west, even when it went forth in great strength and was inspired by all the enthusiasm of a Crusade.

The array of a feudal force was confined to a single pattern. As it was impossible to combine the movements of many small bodies when the troops were neither disciplined nor accustomed to act together, it was usual to form the whole of the cavalry into three great masses, or "battles," as they were called, and launch them at the enemy. The refinement of keeping a reserve in hand was practiced by a few commanders, but these were men distinctly in advance of their age. Indeed, it would often have been hard to persuade a feudal chief to take a position out of the front line and to incur the risk of losing his share in the hard fighting. When two "battles" met, a fearful melee ensued, and would often be continued for hours. Sometimes, as if by agreement, the two parties wheeled to the rear, to give their horses breath, and then rushed at each other again, to renew the conflict till one side grew overmatched and left the field. An engagement like Brémule (A.D. 1119) or Bouvines (A.D. 1214) or Benevento (A.D. 1266) was nothing more than a huge scuffle and scramble of horses and men over a convenient heath or hillside. The most ordinary precautions, such as directing a reserve on a critical point, or detaching a corps to take the enemy in flank, or selecting a good position in which to receive battle, were considered instances of surpassing military skill. Charles of Anjou, for instance, has received the name of a great commander because at Tagliacozzo (A.D. 1268) he retained a body of knights under cover and launched it against Conradin's rear when the Ghibellines had dispersed in pursuit of the routed Angevin main "battle." Simon de Montfort earned high repute; but if at Lewes (A.D. 1264) he kept and utilized a reserve, we must not forget that at Evesham (A.D. 1265) he allowed himself to be surprised and forced to fight with his back to a river, in a position from which no retreat was possible. The commendation of the age was, in short, the meed of striking feats of arms rather than of real generalship. If much attention were to be paid to the chroniclers, we should believe that commanders of merit were numerous; but if we examine the actions of these much-belauded individuals rather than the opinions of their contemporaries, our belief in their ability almost invariably receives a rude shock.[1]

If the minor operations of war were badly understood, strategy—the higher branch of the military art—was absolutely nonexistent.[2] An invading army moved into hostile territory, not in order to strike at some great strategical point, but merely to burn and harry the land. As no organized commissariat existed, the resources of even the richest districts were soon exhausted, and the invader moved off in search of subsistence, rather than for any higher aim. It is only toward the end of the period with which we are dealing that any traces of systematic arrangements for the provisioning of an army are found. Even

[1] Eustace de Ribeaumont, for instance, who gave the madly impractical advice which lost the battle of Poitiers, was, we are told, an officer of high ability.

[2] This is still the generally accepted view of the mediaeval concept of war. However, a more critical study of the generalship of the Middle Ages leads to the conclusion that a real grasp of strategic principles was evidenced by many mediaeval generals. See, for instance, J. H. Round, *Geoffrey de Mandeville* (London, 1892) and Sidney Painter, *The Reign of King John* (Baltimore, 1949). This whole aspect of mediaeval warfare should be thoroughly restudied.

these were for the most part the results of sheer necessity: in attacking a poor and uncultivated territory, like Wales or Scotland, the English kings found that they could not live on the country, and were compelled to take measures to keep their troops from starvation. But a French or German army when it entered Flanders or Lombardy, or an English force in France, trusted, as all facts unite to demonstrate, for its maintenance to its power of plundering the invaded district.[3]

Great battles were, on the whole, infrequent, a fact which appears strange when the long-continued wars of the period are taken into consideration. Whole years of hostilities produced only a few partial skirmishes; compared with modern campaigns, the general engagements were incredibly few. Frederick the Great or Napoleon I fought more battles in one year than a mediaeval commander in ten. The fact would appear to be that the opposing armies, being guided by no very definite aims and invariably neglecting to keep in touch with each other by means of outposts and vedettes, might often miss each other altogether. When they met it was usually from the existence of some topographical necessity, of an old Roman road, or a ford or bridge on which all routes converged. Nothing could show the primitive state of the military art better than the fact that generals solemnly sent and accepted challenges to meet in battle at a given place and on a given day. Without such precautions there was apparently a danger lest the armies should lose sight of each other and stray away in

[3] The Black Prince's campaign in southern France, for example, before the battle of Poitiers, was merely an enormous and destructive raid. He besieged no important town and did not attempt to establish any posts to command the country through which he passed.

different directions. When maps were nonexistent and geographical knowledge was both scanty and inaccurate, this was no inconceivable event.

Even when two forces were actually in presence, it sometimes required more skill than the commanders owned to bring on a battle. Béla IV of Hungary and Ottokar II of Bohemia were in arms in 1260 and both were equally bent on fighting; but when they sighted each other it was only to find that the river March was between them. To pass a stream in the face of an enemy was a task far beyond the ability of the average thirteenth-century general,[4] as St. Louis had found two years earlier on the banks of the Achmoum Canal. Accordingly it was reckoned nothing strange when the Bohemian courteously invited his adversary either to cross the March unhindered, and fight in due form on the west bank, or to give him the same opportunity and grant a free passage to the Hungarian side. Béla chose the former alternative, forded the river without molestation, and fought on the other side the disastrous battle of Kressenbrunn (A.D. 1260).

Infantry was in the twelfth and thirteenth centuries absolutely insignificant: foot soldiers accompanied the army for no better purpose than to perform the menial duties of the camp or to assist in the numerous sieges of the period. Occasionally they were employed as light troops, to open the battle by their ineffective demonstrations. There was, however, no really important part for them to play. Indeed, their lords were sometimes affronted if they presumed

[4] The difficulty experienced by Edward III and Henry V in crossing the Somme is equally remarkable. But Simon de Montfort successfully passed the Severn in the presence of the army of Prince Edward in 1265, and even so incompetent a general as Edward II passed the Bannockburn in the face of the Scots in A.D. 1314.

to delay too long the opening of the cavalry charges, and ended the skirmishing by riding into and over their wretched followers. At Bouvines the Count of Boulogne could find no better use for his infantry than to form them into a great circle, inside which he and his horsemen took shelter when their chargers were fatigued and needed a short rest.[5] If great bodies of foot occasionally appeared upon the field, they came because it was the duty of every able-bodied man to join the *arrière-ban* when summoned, not because the addition of 20,000 or 100,000 half-armed peasants and burghers was calculated to increase the real strength of the levy.[6] The chief cause of their military worthlessness may be said to have been the miscellaneous nature of their armament. Troops like the Scottish Lowlanders, with their long spears, or the Saracen auxiliaries of Frederick II, with their crossbows, deserved and obtained some respect on account of the uniformity of their equipment. But with ordinary infantry the case was different; exposed—without discipline and with a miscellaneous assortment of dissimilar weapons—to a cavalry charge, they could not combine to withstand it, but were ridden down and crushed. The few infantry successes which appear toward the end of the period were altogether exceptional in character [and marked the beginning of a new era in warfare]. The infantry of the Great Company in the east beat the Duke of Athens (A.D. 1311), by inducing him to charge with all his men-at-arms into a swamp. [At Cour-

[5] The infantry of Reginald of Boulogne were steady enough, however, to repel the cavalry assaults of the counts of Dreux and Sancerre. The Brabançon mercenaries were the last of the imperial army to maintain the battle and were cut to pieces by overwhelming numbers. See Oman, *Art of War,* I, 487–88.

[6] These figures are hopelessly exaggerated, as usual.

trai (July 11, 1302), however, the victory was secured by the Flemings, who sturdily received the charge of the French cavalry and then thrust them back into the little stream which Robert of Artois had been rash enough to cross in the face of a determined enemy.]

The attempt to introduce some degree of efficiency into a feudal force drove monarchs to various expedients. Frederick Barbarossa strove to enforce discipline by a strict code of camp laws, an undertaking in which he won no great success, if we may judge of their observance by certain recorded incidents. In 1158, for example, Egbert von Buten, a young Austrian noble, left his post and started off with a thousand men to endeavor to seize one of the gates of Milan, a presumptuous violation of orders in which he lost his life. This was only in accordance with the spirit of the times, and by no means exceptional. If the stern and imposing personality of the great emperor could not win obedience, the task was hopeless for weaker rulers.

Most monarchs were driven into the use of another description of troops, inferior in morale to the feudal force but more amenable to discipline.[7] The mercenary came to the fore in the second half of the twelfth century. A stranger to all the nobler incentives to valor, an enemy to his God and his neighbor, the most deservedly hated man in Europe, he was yet the instrument which kings, even those of the better sort, were obliged to seek out and cherish. When wars ceased to be mere frontier raids and were carried on for long periods at a great distance from the homes

[7] This is a misconception. The mercenaries of Stephen and John proved more faithful, so long as their salaries were paid, than did the feudal baronage. Mercenary troops did not seek needless fights, but there is nothing to indicate that they were inferior in courage or morale to any soldiers of the period.

of most of the baronage, it became impossible to rely on the services of the feudal levy. But how to provide the large sums necessary for the payment of mercenaries was not always obvious. Notable among the expedients employed was that of Henry II of England, who substituted for the personal service of each knight the system of scutage. By this the majority of the tenants of the crown compounded for their personal service by paying two marks for each knight's fee.[8] Thus the king was enabled to pass the seas at the head of a force of mercenaries who were, for most military purposes, infinitely preferable to the feudal array.[9] However objectionable the hired foreigner might be, on the score of his greed and ferocity, he could, at least, be trusted to stand by his colors as long as he was regularly paid. Every ruler found him a necessity in time of war, but to the unconstitutional and oppressive ruler his existence was especially profitable: it was solely by the lavish use of mercenaries that the warlike nobility could be held in check. Despotism could only begin when the monarch became able to surround himself with a strong force of men whose desires and feelings were alien to those of the nation. The tyrant in mediaeval Europe, as in ancient Greece, found his natural support in foreign, hired soldiery. King John, when he drew to himself his *routiers*, Brabanters, and satellites, was unconsciously imitating Pisistratus and Polycrates.

[8] The charge upon the knight's fee varied. There is important evidence also that scutage is far older than the reign of Henry II. It can in fact be traced back to the last year of the eleventh century. See Stenton, *First Century of English Feudalism,* pp. 177–178.

[9] *Capitales barones suos cum paucis secum duxit, solidarios vero milites innumeros* (*The Chronicle of Robert of Torigni* [*Robert de Monte*], ed. Richard Howlett, Vol. IV of *Chronicles of the Reigns of Stephen, Henry II, and Richard I* [Rolls Series; London, 1886], *sub anno* 1159).

The military efficiency of the mercenary of the thirteenth century was, however, only a development of that of the ordinary feudal cavalier. Like the latter, he was a heavily armed horseman; his rise did not bring with it any radical change in the methods of war. Though he was a more practiced warrior, he still worked on the old system—or want of system—which characterized the cavalry tactics of the time.

The final stage in the history of mercenary troops was reached when the bands which had served through a long war, instead of dispersing at its conclusion, held together and moved across the continent in search of a state which might be willing to buy their services. But the age of the Great Company and the Italian *condottieri* lies rather in the fourteenth than the thirteenth century, and its discussion must be deferred to another chapter.

In the whole military history of the period the most striking features are undoubtedly the importance of fortified places and the ascendancy assumed by the defensive in poliorcetics. If battles were few, sieges were numerous and abnormally lengthy. The castle was as integral a part of feudal organization as the mailed knight, and just as the noble continued to heap defense after defense on to the persons of himself and his charger, so he continued to surround his dwelling with more and more fortifications. The simple Norman castle of the eleventh century, with its earthen ramparts and palisaded banks, developed into an elaborate system of concentric works, like those of Caerphilly and of Caernarvon. The walls of the town rivaled those of the citadel, and every country bristled with forts and places of strength, large and small. The one particular in which real military capacity is displayed in the period is the choice of commanding sites for fortresses. A single stronghold was often so well placed that it served as the key to an entire district. The best claim to the possession of a general's eye which can be made in behalf of Richard I rests on the fact that he chose the position for Château Gaillard, the great castle which sufficed to protect the whole of eastern Normandy as long as it was adequately held.

The strength of a mediaeval fortress lay in the extraordinary solidity of its construction. Against walls fifteen to thirty feet thick, the feeble siege artillery of the day— *perrières*, catapults, and trebuchets,—beat without perceptible effect. A Norman keep, solid and tall, with no woodwork to be set on fire and no openings near the ground to be battered in, had an almost endless capacity for passive resistance. Even a weak garrison could hold out as long as its provisions lasted. Mining was perhaps the device which had most hope of success against such a stronghold; [10] but if the castle was provided with a deep moat, or was built directly on a rock, mining was of no avail. There remained the laborious expedient of demolishing the lower parts of the walls by approaches made under cover of a penthouse, or "cat," as it was called. If the moat could be filled, and the cat brought close to the foot of the fortifications, this method might be of some use against a fortress of the simple Norman type. Before bastions were invented, there was no means by which the missiles of the besieged could adequately command the ground immediately below the ramparts. If the defenders showed themselves over the walls—as would be necessary in order to reach men per-

---

[10] The classical instances of the successful employment of the mine in England are the captures of Rochester Castle in 1215 and Bedford Castle in 1224, both works of enormous labor.

pendicularly below them—they were at once exposed to the archers and crossbowmen who, under cover of mantelets, protected the working of the besieger's pioneers. Hence something might be done by the method of demolishing the lower parts of the walls, but the process was always slow, laborious, and exceedingly costly in the matter of human lives. Unless pressed for time, a good commander would almost invariably prefer to starve out a garrison.

The success—however partial and hard won—of this form of attack led to several developments on the part of the defense. The moat was sometimes strengthened with palisading; occasionally small detached forts were constructed just outside the walls on any favorable spot. But the most generally used expedients were the brattice (*bretêche*) and the construction of large towers projecting from the wall and flanking the long stretches of curtain wall which had been found the weak point in the Norman system of fortification. The brattice was a wooden gallery fitted with apertures in its floor, and running along the top of the wall, from which it projected several feet. It was supported by beams built out from the rampart, and commanded, by means of its apertures, the ground immediately at the foot of the walls. Thus the besieger could no longer get out of the range of the missiles of the besieged, and was exposed to them, however close he drew to the fortifications. The objection to the brattice was that, being wooden, it could be set on fire by inflammatory substances projected by the catapults of the besieger. It was therefore superseded ere long by the use of machicolation, where a projecting stone gallery replaced the woodwork.

Far more important was the utilization of the flanking

action of towers,[11] the other great improvement made by
the defense. This rendered it possible to direct a converg-
ing fire from the sides on the point selected for attack by
the besieger. The towers also served to cut off a captured
stretch of wall from any communication with the rest of
the fortifications. By closing the ironbound doors in the
two on each side of the breach, the enemy was left isolated
on the piece of wall he had won, and could not push to right
or left without storming a tower. This development of the
defensive again reduced the offensive to impotence. Starvation was the only weapon likely to reduce a well-defended
place, and fortresses were therefore blockaded rather than
attacked. The besieger, having built a line of circumvalla-
tion and an entrenched camp, sat down to wait for hunger
to do its work.[12] It will be observed that by fortifying his
position he gave himself the advantage of the defensive in
repelling attacks of relieving armies. His other expedients,
such as endeavors to fire the internal buildings of the invested place, to cut off its water supply, or to carry it by
nocturnal escalade, were seldom of much avail.

The number and strength of the fortified places of western Europe explain the apparent futility of many campaigns of the period. A land could not be conquered with
rapidity when every district was guarded by three or four
castles and walled towns, which would each need several
months' siege before they could be reduced. Campaigns
tended either to become plundering raids, which left the
strongholds alone, or to be occupied in the prolonged

[11] A revival of the old Roman system of fortification.
[12] As, for example, did Edward III before Calais. He fortified all
approaches passable for a relieving army, and waited quietly in his
lines.

blockade of a single fortified place. The invention of gun-powder was the first advantage thrown on the side of the attack for three centuries. Even cannon, however, were at the period of their invention, and for long years after-ward, of very little practical importance. The taking of Constantinople (A.D. 1453) by Mahomet II is perhaps the first event of European importance in which the power of artillery played the leading part.

Before proceeding to discuss the rise of the new forms of military efficiency which brought about the end of the supremacy of feudal cavalry, it may be well to cast a glance at those curious military episodes, the Crusades. Consider-ing their extraordinary and abnormal nature, more results might have been expected to follow them than can in fact be traced. When opposed by a system of tactics to which they were unaccustomed, the western nobles were invari-ably disconcerted. At fights such as that of Dorylaeum (A.D. 1097) they were preserved from disaster only by their indomitable energy; tactically beaten, they extricated themselves by sheer hard fighting. On fairly disputed fields, such as that of Antioch (A.D. 1098), they asserted the same superiority over Oriental horsemen which the Byzantine had previously enjoyed. But after a short experi-ence with western tactics the Turks and Saracens fore-swore the battlefield. They normally acted in great bodies of light cavalry, moving rapidly from point to point, and cutting off convoys or attacking detached parties. The Cru-saders were seldom granted, in the twelfth century, those pitched battles which they craved. The Mohammedan leaders would only fight when they had placed all the ad-vantages on their own side; normally they declined the contest. In the east, just as in Europe, the war was one of sieges: armies considered vast by the standards of thirteenth-century Europeans were arrested before the walls of a second-class fortress such as Acre, and, in despair at reducing it by their operations, had to resort to the lengthy process of starving out the garrison. On the other hand, nothing but the ascendancy enjoyed by the defensive could have protracted the existence of the "Kingdom of Jerusalem" when it had sunk to a chain of isolated fortresses dotting the shore of the Levant from Alexandretta to Acre and Jaffa.

If we can point to any modifications introduced into European warfare by the eastern experience of the Crusaders, they are not, with the exception of improvements in fortification, of any great importance. Greek fire, if its composition was really ascertained, would seem to have had very little use in the west; the horse bowman, copied from the cavalry of the Turkish and Mameluke sultans, did not prove a great military success; the adoption of the curved sabre, the "Morris-pike," the horseman's mace,[13] and a few other weapons is hardly worth mentioning. On the whole, the military results of the Crusades were curiously small. As lessons they were wholly disregarded by the European world. When, after the interval of 150 years, a western army once more faced an Oriental foe, it committed at Nicopolis (A.D. 1396) exactly the same blunder which led to the loss of the day at El Mansûra.

[13] This was borrowed either from the Byzantine or the Saracen; it is quite distinct from the rude club occasionally found in the west at an earlier date, as, for example, in the hands of Bishop Odo at Hastings.

CHAPTER V

The Swiss

A.D. 1315-1515

FROM THE BATTLE OF MORGARTEN
TO THE BATTLE OF MARIGNANO

Character, Arms, and Organization

IN THE fourteenth century infantry, after a thousand years of depression and neglect, at last regained its due share of military importance. Almost simultaneously there appeared two peoples asserting a mastery in European politics by the efficiency of their foot soldiery. Their manners of fighting were as different as their national character and geographical position, but although they never met either in peace or war, they were practically allied for the destruction of feudal chivalry. The knight, who had for so long ridden roughshod over the populations of Europe, was now to recognize his masters in the art of war. The free yeomanry of England and the free herdsmen of the Alps were about to enter on their career of conquest.

When war is reduced to its simplest elements, we find that there are only two ways in which an enemy can be met and defeated. Either the shock or the missile must be employed against him. In the one case the victor achieves success by throwing himself on his opponent and worsting him in a hand-to-hand struggle by his numbers, his weight, the superiority of his arms, or the greater strength and skill with which he wields them. In the second case he wins the day by keeping up such a constant and deadly rain of missiles that his enemy is destroyed or driven back before he can come to close quarters. Each of these methods can be combined with the use of very different arms and tactics, and is susceptible of innumerable variations. In the course of history they have alternately asserted their preponderance: in the early Middle Ages shock tactics were entirely in the ascendant, to be succeeded by the missile in the first centuries of the modern era, [and to be once again employed in the mechanized warfare of the twentieth century].

The English archer and the Swiss pikeman represented these two great forms of military efficiency in their simplest and most elementary shapes. The one relied on his power to defeat his enemy's attack by rapid and accurate shooting. The other was capable of driving before him far superior numbers by the irresistible impact and steady pressure of his solid column with its serried hedge of spear points. When tried against the mailclad cavalry which had previously held the ascendancy in Europe, each of these methods was found adequate to secure the victory for those who employed it. Hence the whole military system of the Middle Ages received a profound modification. To the unquestioned predominance of a single form, that of the charge delivered by cavalry, succeeded a rapid alternation of successful and unsuccessful experiments in the correlation and combination of cavalry and infantry, of shock tactics and missile tactics. Further complicated by the results of the introduction of firearms, this struggle has been prolonged down to the present day.

The Swiss of the fourteenth and fifteenth centuries have been compared with much aptness to the Romans of the early Republic. In the Swiss, as in the Roman, character we find the most intense patriotism combined with an utter want of moral sense and a certain meanness and pettiness of conception which prevent us from calling either nation truly great. In both the steadiest courage and the fervor of the noblest self-sacrifice were allied to an appalling ferocity and a cynical contempt and pitiless disregard for the rights of others. Among each people the warlike pride generated by successful wars of independence led ere long to wars of conquest and plunder. As neighbors, both were rendered insufferable by their haughtiness and proneness to take offense on the slightest provocation.[1] As enemies, both were distinguished for their deliberate and cold-blooded cruelty. The resolution to give no quarter, which appears almost pardonable in patriots desperately defending their native soil, becomes brutal when retained in wars of aggression, but reaches the climax of fiendish inhumanity when the slayer is a mere mercenary, fighting for a cause in which he has no national interest. Repulsive as was the bloodthirstiness of the Roman, it was far from equaling in moral guilt the needless ferocity displayed by

---

[1] See, for example, the case cited in C. von Elgger, *Kriegswesen und Kriegskunst der schweizerischen Eidgenossen im* 14., 15., *und* 16. *Jahrhundert* (Lucerne, 1873), where a patrician of Constance having refused to accept a Bernese plappert (small coin) in payment of a wager, and having scornfully called the bear represented on it a cow, the Confederates took the matter up as a national insult, and ravaged the territory of Constance without any declaration of war.

the hired Swiss soldiery on many a battlefield of the six-teenth century.[2]

In no point do we find a greater resemblance between the histories of the two peoples than in the causes of their success in war. Rome and Switzerland alike are examples of the fact that a good military organization and a sound system of national tactics are the surest bases for a sus-tained career of conquest. Provided with these, a vigorous state needs no unbroken series of great commanders. A succession of respectable mediocrities suffices to guide the great engine of war, which works almost automatically and seldom fails to cleave its way to success. The elected con-suls of Rome, the elected or nominated captains of the Confederates, could never have led their troops to victory had it not been for the systems which the experience of their predecessors had brought to perfection. The combina-tion of pliability and solid strength in the legion, the powers of rapid movement and irresistible impact which met in the Swiss column, were competent to win a field without the exertion of any extraordinary ability by the generals who set them in motion.

The battle array which the Confederates invariably em-ployed was one whose prototype had been seen in the Macedonian phalanx. It was always in masses of enormous depth that they presented themselves on the battlefield. Their great national weapon in the days of their highest reputation was the pike, an ashen shaft eighteen feet long fitted with a head of steel which added another foot to its length. It was grasped with two hands widely extended, and was poised at the level of the shoulder with the point

[2] At Novara, for instance, they put to death after the battle sev-eral hundred German prisoners.

slightly sunk, so as to deliver a downward thrust.[3] Before the line projected not only the pikes of the front rank but those of the second, third, and fourth, an impenetrable hedge of bristling points. The men in the interior of the column held their weapons upright until called upon to step forward in order to replace those who had fallen in the foremost ranks. Thus the pikes, rising many feet above the heads of the men who bore them, gave to the charging mass the appearance of a moving wood. Above the phalanx floated numberless flags—the pennons of districts, towns, and guilds,[4] the banners of the cantons, sometimes the great standard of the Ancient League of High Germany, the white cross on the red ground.

The pike, however, was not the only weapon of the Swiss. In the earlier days of their independence, when the Confederacy consisted of three or four cantons, the halberd was their favorite arm, and even in the sixteenth century a considerable proportion of the army continued to employ it. Eight feet in length—with a heavy head which ended in a sharp point and bore on its front a blade like that of a hatchet, on its back a strong hook—the halberd was the most murderous, if also the most ponderous, of weapons. Swung by the strong arms of the Alpine herdsmen, it would cleave helmet, shield, or coat of mail like pasteboard. The sight of the ghastly wounds which it inflicted

---

[3] A late but graphic source is Blaise de Montluc, *Commentaires* in *Collection complète des mémoires relatifs à L'histoire de France* (Paris, 1821–1822), XX–XXII, especially XXI, 27 ff.

[4] At Morat the contingent of Bern alone brought with them (besides the great standard of the canton) the flags of 24 towns and districts (Thun, Aarau, Lenzburg, Interlaken, Burgdorf, the Haslithal, the Emmenthal, etc.) and of eight craft guilds and six other associations.

might well appal the stoutest foe; he who had once felt its edge required no second stroke. It was the halberd which laid Leopold of Hapsburg dead across his fallen banner at Sempach (A.D. 1386), and struck down Charles of Burgundy—all his face one gash from temple to teeth—in the frozen ditch by Nancy (A.D. 1477).[5]

The halberdiers had their recognized station in the Confederates' battle array. They were drawn up in the center of the column, around the chief banner, which was placed under their care. If the enemy succeeded in checking the onset of the pikemen, it was their duty to pass between the front ranks, which opened out to give them egress, and throw themselves into the fray. They were joined in their charge by the bearers of two-handed swords, morning stars, and Lucerne hammers,[6] all weapons of the most fearful efficiency in a hand-to-hand combat. It was seldom that a hostile force, whether infantry or cavalry, sustained this final attack, when the infuriated Swiss dashed in among them, slashing right and left, sweeping off the legs of horses, and cleaving armor and flesh with the same tremendous blow.

In repelling cavalry charges, however, the halberd was found, owing to its shortness, a far less useful weapon than the pike. The disastrous fight at Arbedo in 1422, where the Swiss, having a large proportion of halberdiers in their

[5] The halberd only differed from the English brown bill in having a spike.

[6] The morning star was a club five feet long, set thickly at its end with iron spikes. It had disappeared by the middle of the fifteenth century. The Lucerne hammer was like a halberd, but had three curved prongs instead of the hatchet blade; it inflicted a horrible, jagged wound.

front rank, were broken by the Milanese gendarmes, was the final cause of the relegation of the halberd to the second phase of the battle. From the first shock of the opposing forces it was banished, being reserved for the melee which afterwards ensued.

Next to its solidity, the most formidable quality of the Swiss infantry was its rapidity of movement. No troops "are ever more expeditious upon a march, and in forming themselves for battle, because they are not overloaded with armour." [7] When emergencies arrived a Confederate army could be raised with extraordinary speed; a people who regarded military glory as the one thing which made life worth living flocked to arms without needing a second summons. The outlying contingents marched day and night in order to reach the mustering place in good time. There was no need to waste days in the weary work of organization when every man stood among his kinsmen and neighbors, beneath the pennon of his native town or valley. The troops of the democratic cantons elected their officers, those of the larger states received leaders appointed by their councils, and then without further delay the army marched to meet the enemy. Thus an invader, however unexpected his attack, might in the course of three or four days find twenty thousand men on his hands. They would often be within a few miles of him before he had heard that a Swiss force was in the field.

In the face of such an army it was impossible for the slowly-moving troops of the fourteenth and fifteenth centuries to execute maneuvers. An attempt to alter the line of battle—as Charles the Rash discovered to his dismay at

[7] Niccolò Machiavelli, *The Art of War* (Albany, 1815), p. 66.

Grandson (A.D. 1476),—was sure to lead to disaster. When once the Confederates were in motion their enemy had to resign himself to fighting in whatever order he found himself at the moment. They always made it their rule to begin the fight, and never to allow themselves to be attacked. The composition of their various columns was settled early on the battle morning, and the men moved off to the field already drawn up in their fighting array. There was no pause needed to draw the army out in line of battle; each phalanx marched on the enemy at a steady but swift pace which covered the ground in an incredibly short time. The solid masses glided forward in perfect order and in deep silence until the war cry burst out in one simultaneous roar and the column dashed itself against the hostile front. The rapidity of the Swiss advance had in it something portentous: the great wood of pikes and halberds came rolling over the brow of some neighboring hill; a moment later it was pursuing its even way toward the front, and then— almost before the opponent had time to realize his position —it was upon him, with its four rows of spear points projecting in front and the impetus of file upon file surging up from the rear.

This power of swift movement was—as Machiavelli observed—the result of the Confederates' determination not to burden themselves with heavy armor. Their abstention from its use was originally due to their poverty alone, but was confirmed by the discovery that a heavy panoply would clog and hamper the efficiency of their national tactics. The normal equipment of the pikeman or halberdier was therefore light, consisting of a steel cap and breastplate alone. Even these were not in universal employment; many of the soldiery trusted the defense of their persons to their weapons, and wore only felt hats and leather jerkins.[8] The use of backplates, arm pieces, and greaves was by no means common; indeed, the men wearing them were often not sufficient in number to form a single rank at the head of the column, the post in which they were always placed. The leaders alone were required to present themselves in full armor; they were therefore obliged to ride while on the march, in order to keep up with their lightly armed followers. When they arrived in sight of the enemy they dismounted and led their men to the charge on foot. A few of the patricians and men of knightly family from Bern were found in the fifteenth century serving as cavalry, but their numbers were absolutely insignificant, a few scores at the most.[9]

Although the strength and pride of the Confederates lay in their pikemen and halberdiers, the light troops were by no means neglected. On occasion they were known to form as much as a fourth of the army, and they never sank below a tenth of the whole number.[10] They were originally armed with the crossbow—the weapon of the fabulous Tell—but even before the great Burgundian war the use of the clumsy firearms of the day was general among them. It was their duty to precede the main body and to endeavor

[8] Machiavelli even says that the pikemen in his day did not wear the steel cap, which was entirely confined to the halberdiers. But this can be shown from other sources to be an exaggeration (Machiavelli, *op. cit.*, p. 65).

[9] John Foster Kirk, *History of Charles the Bold* (Philadelphia, 1864–68), II, 288–289.

[10] At Morat, they were nearly a third, 10,000 out of 35,000. At Arbedo they were a seventh; among the Confederates who joined Charles VIII in his march to Naples, only a tenth of the force (Philippe de Commynes, *Mémoires,* ed. Joseph Calmette [Paris, 1924–25], II, 119).

to draw on themselves the attention of the enemy's artillery
and light troops, so that the columns behind them might
advance as far as possible without being molested. Thus
the true use of a line of skirmishers was already appreci-
ated among the Swiss in the fifteenth century. When the
pikemen had come up with them, they retired into the intervals between the various masses and took no part in the
great charge, for which their weapons were not adapted.

It is at once evident that in the simplicity of its com-
ponent elements lay one of the chief sources of the strength
of a Confederate army. Its commanders were not troubled
by any of those problems as to the correlation and subordi-
nation of the various arms which led to so many unhappy
experiments among the generals of other nations. Cavalry
and artillery were practically nonexistent; nor were the
operations hampered by the necessity of finding some employment for those masses of troops of inferior quality who
so often increased the numbers, but not the efficiency, of
a mediaeval army. A Swiss force—however hastily gathered—was always homogeneous and coherent; there was
no residuum of untried or disloyal soldiery for whose conduct special precautions would have to be taken. The larger
proportion of the men among a nation devoted to war had
seen a considerable amount of service; if local jealousies
were ever remembered in the field, they only served to
spur the rival contingents on to a healthy emulation in valor.
However much the cantons might wrangle among themselves, they were always found united against a foreign
attack.[11]

---

[11] E.g., the Forest Cantons were bitterly opposed to the Bernese
policy of engaging in war with Charles the Rash, but their troops
did no worse service than the rest at Grandson or Morat.

Tactics and Strategy

The character and organization of the Confederate army were exceedingly unfavorable to the rise of great generals. The soldier rested his hope of success rather on an entire confidence in the fighting power of himself and his comrades than on the skill of his commander. Troops who have proved in a hundred fields their ability to bear up against the most overwhelming odds are comparatively indifferent as to the personality of their leader. If he is competent, they work out his plan with success; if not, they cheerfully set themselves to repair his faults by sheer hard fighting. Another consideration was even more important among the Swiss: there was a universal prejudice felt against placing the troops of one canton under the orders of the citizen of another. So strong was this feeling that an extraordinary result ensued: the appointment of a commander in chief remained, throughout the brilliant period of Swiss history, an exception rather than the rule. Neither in the time of Sempach, in the old war of Zurich, in the great struggle with Burgundy, nor in the Swabian campaign against Maximilian of Austria was any single general entrusted with supreme authority.[12] The conduct of affairs was in the hands of a council of war, but it was a council which, contrary to the old proverb about such bodies, was always ready and willing to fight. It was composed of the captains

[12] Rudolf von Erlach's position as commander in chief at Laupen was quite exceptional. If we hear in the cases mentioned above of Swiss commanders, we must remember that they were co-ordinate authorities, among whom one man might exert more influence than another, but only by his personal ascendancy, not by legal right. It is a mistake to say that René of Lorraine formally commanded at Morat or Nancy.

of each cantonal contingent, and settled the questions which came under discussion by a simple majority of voices. Before a battle it entrusted the command of van, rear, main body, and light troops to different officers, but the holders of such posts enjoyed a mere delegated authority, which expired with the cessation of the emergency.

The existence of this curious subdivision of power, to which the nearest parallel would be found in early Byzantine days, would suffice by itself to explain the lack of all strategical skill and unity of purpose which was observable in Swiss warfare. The compromise which forms the mean between several rival schemes usually combines their faults, not their merits. But in addition to this, we may suspect that to find any one Swiss officer capable of working out a coherent plan of campaign would have been difficult. The captain was an old soldier who had won distinction on bygone battlefields, but except in his experience he was not different from the men under his orders. Of elaborating the more difficult strategical combinations a Swiss council of war was not much more capable than an average party of veteran sergeant majors would be in our own day.

With tactics, however, the case was different. The best means of adapting the attack in column to the accidents of locality or the quality and armament of the opposing troops were studied in the school of experience. A real tactical system was developed whose efficiency was proved again and again in the battles of the fifteenth century. For dealing with the mediaeval men at arms and infantry against whom it had been designed, the Swiss method was unrivaled; it was only when a new age introduced different conditions into war that it gradually became obsolete.

The normal order of battle employed by the Confederates, however small or large their army might be, was an advance in an echelon of three divisions.[13] The first corps (*vorhut*), that which had formed the van while the force was on the march, made for a given point in the enemy's line. The second corps (*gewaltshaufen*), instead of coming up in line with the first, advanced parallel to it, but at a short distance to its right or left rear. The third corps (*nachhut*) advanced still farther back, and often halted until the effect of the first attack was seen, in order that it might be able to act, if necessary, as a reserve. This disposition left a clear space behind each column, so that if it was repulsed it could retire without throwing into disorder the rest of the army. Other nations (e.g., the French at Agincourt), who were in the habit of placing one corps directly in front of another, had often to pay the penalty for their tactical crime by seeing the defeat of their first line entail the rout of the whole army, each division being rolled back in confusion on that immediately in its rear. The Swiss order of attack had another strong point in rendering it almost impossible for the enemy's troops to wheel inward and attack the most advanced column; if they did so, they at once exposed their own flank to the second column, which was just coming up and commencing its charge.

The advance in echelon of columns was not the only form employed by the Confederates. At Laupen (A.D. 1339) the center or *gewaltshaufen* moved forward and opened

[13] Machiavelli has a very clear account of this form of advance (*op. cit.*, Bk. III, pp. 113–147).

the fight before the wings were engaged. At the combat of Frastenz in 1499, on the other hand, the wings commenced the onset, while the center was refused, and only came up to complete the overthrow.

Even the traditional array in three masses was sometimes discarded for a different formation. At Sempach (A.D. 1386) the men of the Forest Cantons were drawn up in a single wedge (*Keil*). This order was not, as might be expected from its name, triangular, but merely a column of more than ordinary depth in proportion to its frontage. Its object was to break a hostile line of unusual firmness by a concentrated shock delivered against its center. In 1468, during the fighting which preceded the siege of Waldshut, the whole Confederate army moved out to meet the Austrian cavalry in a great hollow square, in the midst of which were placed the banners with their escort of halberdiers. When such a body was attacked, the men faced outward to receive the onset of the horsemen; this they called "forming the hedgehog." [14] So steady were they that, with very inferior numbers, they could face the most energetic charge; in the Swabian war of 1498, 600 men of Zurich, caught in the open plain by 1,000 imperial men-at-arms, "formed a hedgehog, and drove off the enemy with ease and much jesting." [15] Machiavelli speaks of another Swiss order of battle which he calls the Cross; "betwixt the arms of which they place their musketeers, to shelter them from the first shock of an enemy." [16] His description, however, is anything but explicit, and no trace of any formation of the kind in any recorded engagement can be found.

[14] See Elgger, *op. cit.*, p. 280.   [15] *Ibid.*
[16] Machiavelli, *op. cit.*, p. 99.

Development of Swiss Military Supremacy

The first victory of the Confederates was won, not by the tactics which afterwards rendered them famous, but by a judicious choice of a battlefield. Morgarten (A.D. 1315) was a fearful example of the normal uselessness of feudal cavalry in a mountainous country. On a frosty November day, when the roads were like ice underfoot, Leopold of Austria thrust his long, narrow column into the defiles leading to the valley of Schwyz. In front rode the knights, who had of course claimed the honor of opening the contest, while the infantry of four or five thousand blocked the way behind. In the narrow pass of Morgarten, where the road runs between a precipitous slope on the left and the waters of the Egeri lake on the right, the 1,500 Confederates awaited the Austrians. Full of the carelessness which accompanies overweening arrogance, the duke had neglected the most ordinary precaution of exploring his road. He discovered the vicinity of the enemy when a shower of boulders and tree trunks hurtled down the slope on his left flank, where a party of Swiss were posted above, in a position entirely inaccessible to horsemen. A moment later the head of the helpless column was charged by the main body of the mountaineers.

Before the Austrians had realized that the battle had commenced, the halberds and morning stars of the Confederates were working havoc in their van. The front ranks of the knights, wedged so tightly together by the impact of the enemy that they could not lay their lances in rest, much less spur their horses to the charge, fought and died. The center and rear were compelled to halt and stand motionless, unable to push forward on account of the narrowness of the pass or to retreat on account of the infantry, who choked the road behind. For a short time they endured the deadly shower of rocks and logs, which continued to bound down the slope, tear through the crowded ranks, and hurl man and horse into the lake below. Then, by a simultaneous impulse, the greater part of the mass turned their reins and made for the rear. In the press hundreds were pushed over the ridge of the road, to drown in the deep water on the left. The main body burst into the column of their own infantry, and, trampling down their unfortunate followers, fled with such speed as was possible on the slippery path.

The Swiss, having now exterminated the few knights in the van who had remained to fight, came down on the rear of the panic-stricken crowd, and cut down horseman and footman alike without meeting any resistance. John of Winterthur, a contemporary chronicler, declares:

It was not a battle, but a mere butchery of duke Leopold's men; for the mountain folk slew them like sheep in the shambles: no one gave any quarter, but they cut down all, without distinction, till there were none left to kill. So great was the fierceness of the Confederates that scores of the Austrian footmen, when they saw the bravest knights falling helplessly, threw themselves in panic into the lake, preferring to sink in its depths rather than to fall under the fearful weapons of their enemies.[17]

In short, the Swiss won their freedom because, with instinctive tactical skill, they gave the feudal cavalry no opportunity for attacking them at advantage. "They were lords of the field, because it was they, and not their foe, who settled where the fighting should take place." On the

[17] Quoted at length in Elgger, *op. cit.*

steep and slippery road, where they could not win impetus for their charge, and where the narrowness of the defile prevented them from making use of their superior numbers, the Austrians were helpless. The crushing character of the defeat, however, was due to Leopold's inexcusable carelessness in leaving the way unexplored and suffering himself to be surprised in the fatal trap of the pass.

Morgarten exhibits the Swiss military system in a rudimentary condition. Though won, like all Confederate victories, by the charge of a column, it was the work of the halberd, not of the pike. The latter weapon was not yet in general use among the mountaineers of the three cantons; it was, in fact, never adopted by them to so great an extent as was the case among the Swiss of the lower Alpine lands and Aar Valley, the Bernese, and people of Zurich and Lucerne. The halberd, murderous though it might be, was not an arm whose possession would give an unqualified ascendancy to its wielders; it was the position, not the weapons or the tactics, of the Swiss which won Morgarten. But their second great success bears a far higher military importance.

At Laupen (A.D. 1339) for the first time almost since the days of the Romans, infantry, entirely unsupported by horsemen, ranged on a fair field in the plains, withstood an army complete in all arms and superior in numbers.[18] It was 24 years after Duke Leopold's defeat that the Confederates and their newly allied fellows of Bern met the forces of the Burgundian nobility of the valleys of the Aar and

[18] At Bannockburn, the Scots had made good use of their cavalry, which, though not strong, gave them an advantage wanting to the Swiss at Laupen.

Rhone, mustered by all the feudal chiefs between Alsace
and Lake Leman. Count Gerard of Vallangin, the commander of the baronial army, evidently intended to settle
the day by turning one wing of the enemy and crushing it.
With this object he drew up the whole of his cavalry on
the right of his array, his center and left being entirely
composed of infantry. The Swiss formed the three columns which were henceforth to be their normal order of
battle. They were under a single commander, Rudolf von
Erlach, to whom the credit of having first employed the
formation apparently belongs. The Bernese, who were
mainly armed with pikes, formed the center column. The
wings were drawn back, that on the left being composed
of the men of the three old cantons, who were still employing the halberd as their chief weapon, while the right
was made up of other allies of Bern.

[Erlach allowed the baronial army to begin the advance
up the slope on which the Swiss had taken position. When
the enemy was well committed, he launched his three columns, risking the issue of the day on their ability to carry
all before them. The infantry of the barons proved to be
no match for the Confederates; with a steady impulse the
Bernese pushed it back, trampled down the front ranks,
and drove the rest off the field.] A moment later the Burgundian left suffered the same fate at the hands of the
Swiss right. Then, without wasting time in pursuit, the
two victorious masses turned to aid the men of the Forest
Cantons. Surrounded by a raging flood of horsemen on all
sides, the left column was hard pressed. The halberd,
though inflicting the most ghastly wounds, could not prevent the cavalry from occasionally closing in. Like a
rock, however, the mountaineers withstood the incessant

charges, and succeeded in holding their own for the all-important period during which the hostile infantry was being driven off the field. Then the two successful columns came down on the left and rear of the baronial horsemen and steadily met their charge. Apparently the enemy was already exhausted by his attempt to overcome the men of the Forest Cantons, for, after one vain attempt to ride down the Bernese pikemen, he turned and rode off the field, not without considerable loss, as many of his rear guard were intercepted and driven into the river Sense.

Laupen was neither so bloody nor so dramatic a field as Morgarten, but it is one of three great battles which mark the beginning of a new period in the history of war. Bannockburn had already sounded the same note in the distant west, but for the continent Laupen was the first revelation as to the power of good infantry. The experiment which had been tried a few years before at Cassel (A.D. 1328) and Mons-en-Pévèle (A.D. 1304) with such ill success was renewed with a very different result. The Swiss had accomplished the feat which the Flemings had undertaken with inadequate means and experience. Seven years later a yet more striking lesson was to be administered to feudal chivalry, when the archer faced the knight at Crécy. The mailclad horseman was found unable to break the phalanx of pikes, unable to approach the line from which the deadly arrow reached him, but still the old tradition which gave the most honorable name in war to the mounted man was strong enough to perpetuate for another century the cavalry whose day had really gone by. A system which was so intimately bound up with mediaeval life and ideas could not be destroyed by one or by twenty disasters.

Sempach (A.D. 1386), the third great victory won by the Confederates, shares with the less famous fight of Arbedo a peculiar interest. Both were attempts to break the Swiss column by the adoption of a similar method of attack to that which rendered it so formidable. Leopold the Proud, remembering no doubt the powerlessness of the horsemen which had been shown at Laupen, made his knights dismount, as Edward of England had done with such splendid results thirty years earlier. Perhaps he may have borne in mind a similar order given by his ancestor the emperor Albert, when he fought the Bavarians at Hasenbühl in 1298.

[Sempach was a battle in which two armies made contact before either had time to deploy. It was Duke Leopold, however, who took the initiative in this instance. He had been marching in the usual mediaeval formation of three columns with an army which may have numbered less than 1,500 men-at-arms. He had advanced with his horsemen as far as the hamlet of Hildesrieden, near Sempach, when he ran into the advance of a Swiss force marching to meet him with all speed. Doubtless because the main body of the Swiss were not within supporting distance, the vanguard, composed of Lucerners, halted, contrary to their usual custom, and took up a position in front of Hildesrieden. When Leopold discovered the Swiss he dismounted his "vaward battle," apparently on the theory that by employing the tactics of the enemy, the superior weight of his heavily armored knights and men-at-arms should prove to be the deciding factor. His second and third columns retained their horses for use in a decisive charge when the Swiss should have given way. In the clash which followed, the Lucerners were all but overpowered and began to give ground; and the Austrians appeared certain of victory, when the Swiss main body appeared on the field. Allowing the exhausted men of Lucerne to fall off by the flank, the fresh troops, headed by the contingent of Uri, fell upon the duke's vanguard, which was now pretty well played out, owing to its exertions and to the weight of its armor. The fortunes of the day turned at once, and Duke Leopold, seeing his men reduced to extremity and almost certain victory snatched from his grasp, hastily dismounted his second "battle" and led it forward. However, it advanced in considerable disorder, and before it reached the front line, the Swiss broke through the "vaward battle" and bore down upon him. The duke's rear guard, assuming that the day was lost, turned and rode off the field, leaving Leopold and his knights to be surrounded and cut down almost to the last man. At Laupen, the Swiss had demonstrated that they could beat the knight on his horse in a fair field, and Sempach proved that they could defeat him dismounted also.[19]]

What a better general could do by the employment of Leopold's tactical experiment was shown thirty-seven years later on the field of Arbedo, June 30, 1422. On that occasion Carmagnola, the Milanese general—who then met the Confederates for the first time—opened the engagement with a cavalry charge. Observing its entire failure, the experienced condottiere at once resorted to another form of attack. He dismounted the whole of his 6,000 men-at-arms [20] and launched them in a single column against the Swiss phalanx. The enemy, a body of 4,000

[19] This paragraph has been rewritten from Oman's own revision in *Art of War*, II, 248–252.

[20] This figure is doubtless much exaggerated.

men from Uri, Unterwalden, Zug, and Lucerne, were mainly halberdiers, the pikemen and crossbowmen forming only a third of their force. The two masses met and engaged in a fair duel between lance and sword on the one hand and pike and halberd on the other. The impetus of the larger force bore down that of the smaller, and, in spite of the desperate fighting of their enemies, the Milanese began to gain ground. So hard pressed were the Confederates now that the *Schultheiss* of Lucerne even thought of surrender, and planted his halberd in the ground in token of submission. Carmagnola, however, heated with the fight, cried out that men who gave no quarter should receive none, and continued his advance. He was on the very point of victory,[21] when a new Swiss force suddenly appeared in his rear. Believing them to be the contingents of Zurich, Schwyz, Glarus, and Appenzell, which he knew to be at no great distance, Carmagnola drew off his men and began to reform. But in reality the newcomers were only a band of 600 foragers; they made no attack, while the Swiss main body took advantage of the relaxation of

[21] Sismondi, who writes entirely from Swiss sources as to this fight, gives a very different impression from Machiavelli (J. C. L. Simonde de Sismondi, *Histoire de républiques italiennes du moyen age* [Paris, 1826], VIII, 325–329). The latter cites Arbedo as the best-known check received by the Swiss, and puts their loss down at several thousands (Machiavelli, *op. cit.*, p. 68). Müller evidently tries to minimize the check; but we may judge from our knowledge of Swiss character how great must have been the pressure required to make a Confederate officer think of surrender. Forty-four members of the cantonal councils of Lucerne fell in the fight: "The contingent of Lucerne had crossed the lake of the four Cantons in ten large barges, when setting out on this expedition: it returned in two!" These facts, acknowledged by the Swiss themselves, seem to show that the figure of 400 men for their loss is placed absurdly low.

the pressure to retire in good order. They had lost 400 men according to their own acknowledgment, many more if Italian accounts are to be received. Carmagnola's loss, though numerically larger, bore no such proportion to his whole force, and had indeed been mainly incurred in the unsuccessful cavalry charge which opened the action.

From the results of Sempach and Arbedo it seems natural to draw the conclusion that a judicious employment of dismounted men-at-arms might have led to success if properly combined with the use of other arms. The experiment, however, was never repeated by the enemies of the Swiss; indeed, almost the only consequence which we can attribute to it is a decree of the Council of Lucerne that "since things had not gone altogether well with the Confederates" a larger proportion of the army was in future to be furnished with the pike,[22] a weapon which, unlike the halberd, could contend on superior terms with the lance.

Putting aside the two battles which we have last examined, we may say that for the first 150 years of their career the Swiss were so fortunate as never to meet either with a master of the art of war or with any new form of tactical efficiency which could rival their own phalanx. It was still with the mailed horsemen or the motley and undisciplined infantry array of the Middle Ages that they had to deal. Their tactics had been framed for successful conflict with such forces, and continued to preserve an ascendancy over them. The free lances of Enguerrand de Coucy, the burghers and nobles of Swabia, and the knights who followed Frederick or Leopold or Sigismund of Hapsburg

[22] From a Lucerne *"Raths-Protocoll"* of 1422, *"Da es den Eidgenossen nicht so wohl ergangen seie,"* etc.

were none of them exponents of a new system, and served each in their turn to demonstrate yet more clearly the superiority of the Confederates in military skill.

Even the most dangerous attack ever aimed against Switzerland, the invasion by the Armagnac mercenaries of the Dauphin Louis in 1444, was destined to result in the increase of the warlike reputation of its soldiery. The battle of St. Jacob-en-Birs (A.D. 1444), mad and unnecessary though it was, might serve as an example to deter the boldest enemy from meddling with men who preferred annihilation to retreat. Possessed by the single idea that their phalanx could bear down any obstacle, the Confederates, numbering less than 1,000, deliberately crossed the Birs in face of an army of fifteen times their strength. They attacked it, broke its center, and were then surrounded by its overwhelming numbers. Compelled to form the hedgehog in order to resist the tremendous cavalry charges directed against them, they remained rooted to the spot for the remainder of the day. The dauphin launched squadron after squadron at them, but each in its turn was hurled back in disorder. In the intervals between these onsets the French light troops poured in their missiles, but though the clump of pikes and halberds grew smaller it still remained impenetrable. Not until the evening was the fighting ended, and then 2,000 Armagnacs lay dead around the heap of Swiss corpses in the center. Louis saw that a few such victories would destroy his whole army, and turned back into Alsace, leaving Switzerland unmolested.

From that day the Confederates were able to reckon their reputation for obstinate and invincible courage as one of the chief causes which gave them political importance. The generals and armies who afterwards faced them went

into battle without full confidence in themselves. It was
no light matter to engage with an enemy who would not
retire before any superiority in numbers, who was always
ready for the fight, who would neither give nor take quarter. The enemies of the Swiss found these considerations
the reverse of inspiriting before a combat; it may almost
be said that they came into the field expecting a defeat,
and therefore earned one. This fact is especially noticeable
in the great Burgundian war. If Charles the Rash himself
was unawed by the warlike renown of his enemies,[23] the
same cannot be said of his troops. A large portion of his
motley army could not be trusted in any dangerous crisis:
the German, Italian, and Savoyard mercenaries knew too
well the horrors of Swiss warfare, and shrank instinctively
from the shock of the phalanx of pikes. The duke might
range his men in order of battle, but he could not be
sure that they would fight. The old proverb that "God was
on the side of the Confederates" was ever ringing in their
ears, and so they were half beaten before a blow was struck.
Charles had endeavored to secure the efficiency of his
army by enlisting from each warlike nation of Europe the
class of troops for which it was celebrated. The archers
of England, the arquebusiers of Germany, the light cavalry
of Italy, and the pikemen of Flanders marched side by
side with the feudal chivalry of his Burgundian vassals.
But the duke had forgotten that, in assembling so many
nationalities under his banner, he had thrown away the
cohesion which is all-important in battle. Without mutual
confidence or certainty that each comrade would do his

[23] Yet even the Duke said, that "Against the Swiss it will never
do to march unprepared" (Panagirola, quoted by Kirk, *op. cit.*, III,
276).

best for the common cause, the soldiery would not stand firm. Grandson (A.D. 1476) was lost merely because the nerve of the infantry failed them at the decisive moment, although they had not yet been engaged.

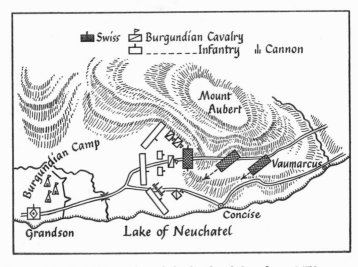

Fig. 2. Military plan of the battle of Grandson, 1476.

In that fight the unskillful generalship of the Swiss had placed the tactical advantages on the side of Charles: he had both outflanked them and attacked one division of their army before the others came up. He had, however, to learn that an army superior in morale and homogeneity, and thoroughly knowing its weapon, may be victorious in spite of all disadvantages. Owing to their eagerness for battle the Confederate vanguard (*vorhut*), composed of the troops of Bern, Fribourg, Schwyz, and Basle, had far outstripped the remainder of the force. Coming swiftly over the hillside in one of their usual deep columns, they found the whole Burgundian army spread out before them in battle array on the plain of Grandson. As they reached the foot of the hill they at once saw that the Duke's cavalry was preparing to attack them. Old experience had made them callous to such sights: facing outward, the column awaited the onset. The first charge was made by the cavalry of Charles' left wing; it failed, although the gallant lord of Chateauguyon, who led it, forced his horse among the pikes and died at the foot of the standard of Schwyz. Next the duke himself led on the lances of his guard, a force who had long been esteemed the best troops in Europe; they did all that brave men could, but were dashed back in confusion from the steady line of spear points.

The Swiss now began to move forward into the plain, eager to try the effect of the impact of their phalanx on the Burgundian line. To meet this advance Charles determined to draw back his center and, when the enemy advanced against it, to wheel both his wings round upon their flank. The maneuver appeared feasible, as the remainder of the Confederate army was not yet in sight. Orders were accordingly sent to the infantry and guns who were immediately facing the approaching column, directing them to retire; at the same time, the reserve was sent to strengthen the left wing, the body with which the duke intended to deliver his most crushing stroke. The Burgundian army was in fact engaged in repeating the movement which had given Hannibal victory at Cannae: his fortune, however, was very different. At the moment when the center had begun to draw back, and when the wings were not yet engaged, the heads of the two Swiss columns, which had not before appeared, came over the brow of Mont Aubert, moving rapidly toward the battlefield with the usual majestic steadiness of their formation. This of course would have frustrated Charles' scheme for surrounding the first phalanx, the echelon of divisions, which was the normal Swiss array, being now established.

The aspect of the fight, however, was changed even more suddenly than might have been expected. Connecting the retreat of their center with the advance of the Swiss, the whole of the infantry of the Burgundian wings broke and fled, long before the Confederate masses had come into contact with them. It was a sheer panic, caused by the fact that the duke's army had no cohesion or confidence in itself; the various corps in the moment of danger could not rely on each other's steadiness, and, seeing what they imagined to be the rout of their center, had no further thought of endeavoring to turn the fortune of the day. It may be said that no general could have foreseen such a disgraceful flight; but at the same time the duke may be censured for attempting a delicate maneuver with an army destitute of homogeneity, and in the face of an enterprising opponent. Strategical movements to the rear have always a tendency to degenerate into undisguised retreats, unless the men are perfectly in hand, and should therefore be avoided as much as possible. Grandson was for the Swiss only one more example of the powerlessness of the best cavalry against their columns; of infantry fighting there was none at all.

In the second great defeat which he suffered at the hands of the Confederates the duke was guilty of far more flagrant faults in his generalship. At the siege of Morat (A.D. 1476) his army was divided into three parts which in the event of a flank attack could bring each other no succor. The position which he had chosen and fortified

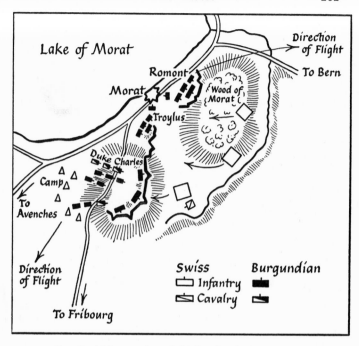

Fig. 3. Military plan of the battle of Morat, 1476.

for the covering of his siege operations only protected them against an assault from the southeast. Still more strange was it that the Burgundian light troops were held back so close to the main body that the duke had no accurate knowledge of the movements of his enemies till they appeared in front of his lines. It was thus possible for the Confederate army to march, under cover of the Wood of Morat, right across the front of the two corps which virtually composed the center and left of Charles' array. As it was well known that the enemy were in the immediate vicinity, it is hard to conceive how the duke could be content to wait in battle order for six hours without sending out troops to obtain information. It is nevertheless certain that when the Swiss did not show themselves, he sent back his main body to camp, and left the carefully entrenched position in the charge of a few thousand men.

Hardly had this fault been committed when the Confederate vanguard appeared on the outskirts of the Wood of Morat and marched straight on the palisade. The utterly inadequate garrison made a bold endeavor to hold their ground, but in a few minutes were driven down the reverse slope of the hill into the arms of the troops who were coming up in hot haste from the camp to their succor. The Swiss following hard in their rear pushed the disordered mass before them, and crushed in detail each supporting corps as it straggled up to attack them. The greater part of the Burgundian infantry turned and fled, with far more excuse than at Grandson. Many of the cavalry corps endeavored to change the fortune of the day by desperate but isolated charges, in which they met the usual fate of those who attempted to break a Swiss phalanx. The fighting, however, was soon at an end, and mere slaughter took its place. While the van and main body of the Confederates followed the flying crowd who made off in the direction of Avenches, the rear came down on the Italian infantry, who had formed the besieging force south of the town of Morat. These unfortunates, whose retreat was cut off by the direction which the flight of the main body had taken, were trodden under foot or pushed into the lake by the impact of the Swiss column, and were almost entirely annihilated, scarcely a single man escaping out of a force of six thousand. The Savoyard corps under Romont, who had composed the duke's extreme left and were posted to the north of Morat, escaped by a hazardous march which took them round the rear of the Confederates.

Though Charles had done his best to prepare a victory for his enemies by the faultiness of his dispositions, the management of the Swiss army at Morat was the cause of the completeness of his overthrow. A successful attack on the Burgundian right would cut off the retreat of the two isolated corps which composed the duke's center and left; the Confederate leaders therefore determined to assault this point, although to reach it they had to march straight across their opponent's front.[24] Favored by his astonishing oversight in leaving their march unobserved, they were able to surprise him and destroy his army in detail before it could manage to form even a rudimentary line of battle.

At Nancy (A.D. 1477) the Swiss commanders again displayed considerable skill in their dispositions: the main "battle" and the small rear column held back and attracted the attention of the Burgundian army while the van executed a turning movement through the woods, which brought it out on the enemy's flank and made his position perfectly untenable. The duke's troops assailed in front and on their right at the same moment, and having to deal with very superior numbers, were not merely defeated but were dispersed or destroyed. Charles himself, refusing to fly, and fighting desperately to cover the retreat of his scattered forces, was surrounded and was cleft through helmet and skull by the tremendous blow of a Swiss halberd.

[24] "If we attack Romont," said Ulrich Kätzy at the Swiss council of war, "while we are beating him the duke will have time and opportunity to escape; let us go round the hills against the main-body, and when that is routed, we shall have the rest without a stroke." This showed real tactical skill.

The generalship displayed at Nancy and Morat was, however, exceptional among the Confederates. After those battles, just as before, we find that their victories continued to be won by a headlong and desperate onset, rather than by the display of any great strategical ability. In the Swabian war of 1499 the credit of their successes falls to the troops rather than to their leaders. The stormings of the fortified camps of Hard and Malsheide were wonderful examples of the power of unshrinking courage; but on each occasion the Swiss officers seem to have considered that they were discharging their whole duty when they led their men straight against the enemy's entrenchments. At Frastenz (A.D. 1499) the day was won by a desperate charge up the face of a cliff which the Tyrolese had left unguarded as being inaccessible. Even at Dornach (A.D. 1499)—the last battle fought on Swiss soil against an invader till the eighteenth century—the fortune of the fight turned on the superiority of the Confederate to the Swabian pikemen man for man and on the fact that the lances of Gueldres could not break the flank column by their most determined onset. Of maneuvering there appears to have been little, and of strategical planning none at all; it was considered sufficient to launch the phalanx against the enemy and trust to its power of bearing down every obstacle that came in its way.

Causes of the Decline of Swiss Ascendancy

Their disregard for the higher and more delicate problems of military science was destined to enfeeble the power and destroy the reputation of the Confederates. At a time when the great struggle in Italy was serving as a school

for the soldiery of other European nations, they alone refused to learn. Broad theories, drawn from the newly discovered works of the ancients, were being co-ordinated
with the modern experience of professional officers and
were developing into an art of war far superior to anything
known in mediaeval times. Scientific engineers and artillerists had begun to modify the conditions of warfare, and
feudal tradition was everywhere discarded. New forms
of military efficiency, such as the sword-and-buckler men
of Spain, the stradiot light cavalry, and the German "black
bands" of musketeers, were coming to the front. The improvement of the firearms placed in the hands of infantry
was only less important than the superior mobility which
was given to field artillery.

The Swiss, however, paid no attention to these changes;
the world around them might alter, but they would hold
fast to the tactics of their ancestors. At first, indeed, their
arms were still crowned with success: they were seen in
Italy, as in more northern lands, to "march with ten or
fifteen thousand [pikemen] against any number of horse,"
and to win a general opinion of their excellence from the
many remarkable services they performed.[25] They enjoyed
for a time supreme importance, and left their mark on the
military history of every nation of central and southern
Europe. But it was impossible that a single stereotyped
tactical method, applied by men destitute of any broad and
scientific knowledge of the art of war, should continue to
assert an undisputed ascendancy. The victories of the Swiss
set every officer of capacity and versatile talent searching
for an efficient way of dealing with the onset of the phalanx.

[25] Machiavelli, *op. cit.*, pp. 65–66.

Such a search was rendered comparatively easy by the fact that the old feudal cavalry and the worthless mediaeval infantry were being rapidly replaced by disciplined troops, men capable of keeping cool and collected even before the desperate rush of the Confederate pikemen. The standing army of Charles of Burgundy had been rendered inefficient by its want of homogeneity and cohesion, as well as by the bad generalship of its leader. The standing armies which fought in Italy thirty years later were very different bodies. Although still raised from among various nations, they were united by the bonds of old comradeship, of *esprit de corps*, of professional pride, or of confidence in some favorite general. The Swiss had therefore to face troops of a far higher military value than they had ever before encountered.

The first experiment tried against the Confederates was that of the emperor Maximilian, who raised in Germany corps of pikemen and halberdiers trained to act in a manner exactly similar to that of their enemies. The *Landsknechte* soon won for themselves a reputation second only to that of the Swiss, whom they boldly met in many a bloody field. The conflicts between them were rendered obstinate by military as well as national rivalry, the Confederates being indignant that any troops should dare to face them with their own peculiar tactics, while the Germans were determined to show that they were not inferior in courage to their Alpine kinsmen. The shock of the contending columns was therefore tremendous. The two bristling lines of pikes crossed, and the leading files were thrust upon each other's weapons by the irresistible pressure from behind. Often the whole front rank of each phalanx went down in the first onset, but their comrades

stepped forward over their bodies to continue the fight.[26]
When the masses had been for some time pushing against
each other, their order became confused and their pikes
interlocked; then was the time for the halberdiers to act.[27]
The columns opened out to let them pass, or they rushed
round from the rear, and threw themselves into the melee.
This was the most deadly epoch of the strife; the combatants mowed each other down with fearful rapidity.
Their ponderous weapons allowed of little fencing and
parrying, and inflicted wounds which were almost invariably mortal. Everyone who missed his blow, or stumbled
over a fallen comrade, or turned to fly was a doomed man.
Quarter was neither expected nor given.

Of course these fearful hand-to-hand combats could not
be of great duration; one party had ere long to give ground
and suffer the most fearful losses in its retreat. It was in a
struggle of this kind that the *Landsknechte* lost a full half
of their strength when the Swiss bore them down at Novara
(A.D. 1513). Even, however, when they were victorious,
the Confederates found that their military ascendancy was
growing less; they could no longer sweep the enemy from
the field by a single unchecked onset, but were confronted
by troops who were ready to turn their own weapons
against them and who required the hardest pressure before
they would give ground. In spite of their defeats the
Landsknechte kept the field, and finally took their revenge

---

[26] Frundsberg, the old captain of *landsknechte,* gives a cool and
businesslike account of these shocks: *Wo unter den langen Wehren
etliche* Glieder *zu grund gehen, werden die Personen, so dahinter
stehen, etwas zaghaft,* etc.

[27] The two-handed sword had almost entirely, and the morning
star and Lucerne hammer quite, disappeared from use by the end
of the fifteenth century.

when the Swiss recoiled in disorder from the fatal trenches of La Bicocca (A.D. 1522).

There was, however, an enemy even more formidable than the German, who was to appear upon the scene at a slightly later date. The Spanish infantry of Gonsalvo de Córdova displayed once more to the military world the strength of the tactics of old Rome. They were armed, like the men of the ancient legion, with the short thrusting sword and buckler, and wore the steel cap, breast- and back-plates, and greaves. Thus they were far stronger in their defensive armor than the Swiss whom they were about to encounter. When the pikeman and the swordsman first met in 1503, under the walls of Barletta, the old problem of Pydna (168 B.C.) and Cynoscephalae (197 B.C.) was once more worked out. A phalanx as solid and efficient as that of Philip the Macedonian was met by troops whose tactics were those of the legionaries of Aemilius Paullus. Then, as in an earlier age, the wielders of the shorter weapon prevailed.

When they came to engage, the Swiss pressed so hard on their enemy with their pikes, that they soon opened their ranks; but the Spaniards, under the cover of their bucklers, nimbly rushed in upon them with their swords, and laid about them so furiously, that they made a very great slaughter of the Swiss, and gained a complete victory.[28]

The vanquished, in fact, suffered at the hands of the Spaniard the treatment which they themselves had inflicted on the Austrians at Sempach. The bearer of the longer weapon becomes helpless when his opponent has closed with him, whether the arms concerned be lance

[28] Machiavelli, *op. cit.*, p. 70.

and halberd or pike and sword. The moment a breach had been made in a Macedonian or Swiss phalanx the great length of their spears became their ruin. There was nothing to do but to drop them, and in the combat which then ensued troops using the sword alone, and without defensive armor, were at a hopeless disadvantage in attacking men furnished with the buckler as well as the sword, and protected by a more complete panoply. Whatever may be the result of a duel between sword and spear alone, it is certain that when a light shield is added to the swordsman's equipment, he at once obtains the ascendancy. The buckler serves to turn aside the spear point, and then the thrusting weapon is free to do its work.[29] It was, therefore, natural that when Spanish and Swiss infantry met, the former should in almost every case obtain success.

The powerlessness of the pike, however, was most strikingly displayed at a battle in which the fortune of the day had not been favorable to Spain. At the fight of Ravenna (A.D. 1512) Gaston de Foix had succeeded in driving Don Ramón de Cardona from his entrenchments, and was endeavoring to secure the fruits of victory by a vigorous pursuit. To intercept the retreat of the Spanish infantry, who were retiring in good order, Gaston sent forward the pikemen of Jacob Empser, then serving as auxiliaries beneath

[29] It is a curious fact that Chaka, one of Cetywayo's predecessors as king of the Zulus, set himself to solve this problem. He took a hundred men and armed them with the shield and the short assagai, a thrusting weapon resembling a sword rather than a spear in its use. He then set them to fight another hundred furnished with the shield and the long assagai, the slender javelin which had previously been the weapon of his tribe. The wielders of the shorter weapon won with ease, and the king thereupon ordered its adoption throughout the Zulu army. It was this change which originally gave the Zulus their superiority over their neighbors.

the French banner. These troops accordingly fell on the retreating column and attempted to arrest its march. The Spaniards, however, turned at once and fell furiously on the Germans, "rushing at the pikes, or throwing themselves on the ground and slipping below the points, so that they darted in among the legs of the pikemen." In this way they succeeded in closing with their opponents, and "made so good a use of their swords, that not one of the enemy would have been left alive, if a body of French cavalry had not fortunately come up to rescue them." [30] This fight was typical of many more in which during the first quarter of the sixteenth century the sword and buckler were proved to be more than master of the pike.

It may, therefore, be asked why, in the face of these facts, the Swiss weapon remained in use, while the Spanish infantry finally discarded their peculiar tactics. To this question the answer is found in the consideration that the sword was not suited for repulsing a cavalry charge, while the pike continued to be used for that purpose down to the invention of the bayonet at the end of the seventeenth century. Machiavelli was, from his studies in Roman antiquity, the most devoted admirer of the Spanish system, which seemed to bring back the days of the ancient legion. Yet even he conceded that the pike, a weapon which he is on every occasion ready to disparage, must be retained by a considerable portion of those ideal armies for whose guidance he drew up his *Art of War*. He could think of no other arm which could resist a charge of cavalry steadily pressed home, and was therefore obliged to combine pikemen with his *velites* and buckler men.

The rapid development of the arts of the engineer and

[30] Machiavelli, *op. cit.*, p. 70.

artillerist aimed another heavy blow at the Swiss supremacy. The many-sided energy of the Renaissance period not infrequently made the professional soldier a scholar and set him to adapt the science of the ancients to the requirements of modern warfare. The most cursory study of Vegetius, Hyginus, or Vitruvius, all of them authors much esteemed at the time, would suffice to show the strength of the Roman fortified camp. Accordingly the art of castrametation revived, and corps of pioneers were attached to every army. It became common to entrench not merely permanent positions, but camps which were to be held for a few days only. Advantage was taken of favorable sites, and lines of greater or less strength with emplacements for artillery were constructed for the protection of the army which felt itself inferior in the field. Many of the greatest battles of the Italian wars were fought in and around such positions; Ravenna, La Bicocca, and Pavia (A.D. 1525) are obvious examples. Still more frequently a general threw himself with all his forces into a fortified town and covered it with outworks and redoubts till it resembled an entrenched camp rather than a mere fortress.

Such a phase in war was most disadvantageous to the Swiss: even the most desperate courage cannot carry men over stone walls or through flooded ditches, if they neglect the art which teaches them how to approach such obstacles. The Confederates in their earlier days had never displayed much skill in attacking places of strength; and now, when the enemy's position was as frequently behind defenses as in the open plain, they refused to adapt their tactics to the altered circumstances. Occasionally, as, for example, at the storming of the outworks of Genoa in 1507, they were still able to sweep the enemy before them by the mere vehemence of their onset. But more frequently disaster followed the headlong rush delivered against lines held by an adequate number of steady troops. Of this the most striking instance was seen in 1522, when the Swiss columns attempted to dislodge the enemy from the fortified park of La Bicocca. Under severe fire from the Spanish hackbuteers they crossed several hedges and flooded trenches which covered the main position of the imperialists. But when they came to the last ditch and bank, along which were ranged the *Landsknechte* of Frundsberg, they found an obstacle which they could not pass. Leaping into the deep excavation, the front ranks endeavored to scramble up its further slope; but every man who made the attempt fell beneath the pike thrusts of the Germans, who, standing on a higher level in their serried ranks, kept back the incessant rushes with the greatest steadiness. Three thousand corpses were left in the ditch before the Swiss would desist from their hopeless undertaking; it was an attack which, for misplaced daring, rivals the British assault on Ticonderoga in 1758.

The improved artillery of the early sixteenth century worked even more havoc with the Confederates. Of all formations the phalanx is the easiest at which to aim, and the one which suffers most loss from each cannon ball which strikes it. A single shot ploughing through its dense ranks might disable 20 men, yet the Swiss persisted in rushing straight for the front of batteries and storming them in spite of their murderous fire. Such conduct might conceivably have been justifiable in the fifteenth century, when the clumsy guns of the day could seldom deliver more than a single discharge between the moment at

which the enemy came within range and that at which
he reached their muzzles. Scientific artillerists, however,
such as Pedro Navarro and Alfonso d'Este, made cannon
a real power in battles by increasing its mobility and the
rapidity of its fire. None the less, the Confederates continued to employ the front attack, which had become four
or five times more dangerous in the space of forty years.
A fearful lesson as to the recklessness of such tactics was
given them at Marignano (A.D. 1515), where, in spite of
the gallantry of the French gendarmerie, it was the artillery
which really won the day. The system which Francis' ad-
visers there employed was to deliver charge after charge
of cavalry on the flanks of the Swiss columns while the
artillery played upon them from the front. The onsets of
the cavalry, though they never succeeded in breaking the
phalanx, forced it to halt and form the hedgehog. The men-
at-arms came on in bodies of about 500 strong, one taking
up the fight when the first had been beaten off. "In this way
more than 30 fine charges were delivered, and no one will
in future be able to say that cavalry are of no more use
than hares in armour," wrote the king to his mother. Of
course these attacks would by themselves have been fruitless; it was the fact that they checked the advance of the
Swiss, and obliged them to stand halted under artillery fire
that settled the result of the battle.[31] At last the columns
had suffered so severely that they gave up the attempt to
advance, and retired in good order, unbroken but diminished by a half in their size.

Last but not least important among the causes of the
decline of the military ascendancy of the Confederates was

[31] Sismondi, *op. cit.*, XIV, 373–379.

the continual deterioration of their discipline. While among other nations the commanders were becoming more and more masters of the art of war, among the Swiss they were growing more and more the slaves of their own soldiery. The division of their authority had always been detrimental to the development of strategical skills, but it now began to make even tactical arrangements impossible. The army looked upon itself as a democracy entitled to direct the proceedings of its ministry, rather than a body under military discipline. Filled with a blind confidence in the invincibility of their onset, they calmly neglected the orders which appeared to them superfluous. On several occasions they delivered an attack on the front of a position which it had been intended to turn; on others they began the conflict, although they had been directed to wait for the arrival of other divisions before giving battle. If things were not going well they threw away even the semblance of obedience to their leaders. Before La Bicocca the cry was raised, "Where are the officers, the pensioners, the double-pay men? Let them come out and earn their money fairly for once: they shall all fight in the front rank to-day." What was even more astonishing than the arrogance of the demand was the fact that it was obeyed. The commanders and captains stepped forward and formed the head of the leading column; hardly one of them survived the fight, and Winkelried of Unterwalden, the leader of the vanguard, was the first to fall under the lances of Frundsberg's *Landsknechte*. What was to be expected from an army in which the men gave the orders and the officers executed them? Brute strength and heedless courage were the only qualities now employed by the Swiss, while against them were pitted the scientific generals of the new school of war. The result was what might have been expected: the pike tactics, which had been the admiration of Europe, were superseded because they had become stereotyped, and the Swiss lost their proud position as the most formidable infantry in the world.

CHAPTER VI

The English and Their Enemies

A.D. 1272-1485

FROM THE ACCESSION OF EDWARD I TO
THE END OF THE WARS OF THE ROSES

THE use of the longbow is as much the key to the successes of the English armies in the fourteenth and fifteenth centuries as that of the pike is to the successes of the Swiss. Dissimilar as were the characters of the two weapons, and the national tactics to which their use led, they were both employed for the same end of terminating the ascendancy in war of the mailed horseman of the feudal regime. It is certainly not the least curious part of the military history of the period that the commanders who made such good use of their archery had no conception of the tendencies of their action. Edward the Black Prince and his father regarded themselves as the flower of chivalry, and would have been horrified had they realized that their own tactics were going far to make chivalrous warfare impossible. Such, however, was the case; that unscientific kind of combat which resembled a huge tilting match could not continue if one side persisted in bringing into the field auxiliaries who could prevent their opponents from approaching near enough to break a lance. The needs of the moment, however, prevented the English commanders being troubled by such thoughts; they made the best use of the material at their disposal, and if they thus found themselves able to beat the enemy, they were satisfied.

It is not till the last quarter of the thirteenth century that we find the longbow taking up its position as the national weapon of England. In the armies of the Norman and Angevin kings, archers were indeed to be found, but they formed neither the most numerous nor the most effective part of the array. On the English side of the Channel, just as beyond it, the supremacy of the mailed horseman was still unquestioned. It is indeed noteworthy that the theory which attributes to the Normans the introduction of the longbow is impossible to substantiate. If we are to trust the Bayeux Tapestry—whose accuracy is in other matters thoroughly borne out by all contemporary evidence—the weapon of William's archers was in no way different from that already known in England, and was used by a few of the English in the fight of Hastings.[1] It is the short bow, drawn to the breast and not to the ear. The bowmen who are occasionally mentioned during the succeeding century, as, for example, those present at the Battle of the Standard (A.D. 1138), do not appear to form any very important part of the national force. Nothing can be more conclusive as to the insignificance of the weapon than the fact that it is not mentioned at all in the Assize of Arms of 1181. In the reign of Henry II, therefore, we may fairly conclude that the bow did not form the proper weapon of any class of English society. A similar deduction is suggested by Richard Coeur de Lion's predilection for the

[1] E.g., by the diminutive archer who crouches under a thegn's shield, like Teucer protected by Ajax.

arbalest; it is impossible that he should have introduced that weapon as a new and superior arm if he had been acquainted with the splendid longbow of the fourteenth century. It is evident that the bow must always preserve an advantage in rapidity of fire over the arbalest; the latter must therefore have been considered by Richard to surpass in range and penetrating power. But nothing is better established than the fact that the trained archer of the Hundred Years' War was able to beat the crossbowmen on both these points. It is, therefore, rational to conclude that the weapon superseded by the arbalest was merely the old short bow, which had been in constant use since Saxon times.

However this may be, the crossbowmen continued to occupy the first place among light troops during the reigns of Richard and John. The former monarch devised for them a system of tactics in which the pavis was made to play a prominent part. The latter entertained great numbers of both horse and foot arbalesters among those mercenary bands who were such a scourge to England. It would appear that the barons, in their contest with John, suffered greatly from having no adequate provision of infantry armed with missiles to oppose the crossbowmen of Fawkes de Breauté and his fellows. Even in the reign of Henry III, the epoch in which the longbow begins to come into use, the arbalest was still reckoned the more effective arm. In 1242, at the battle of Taillebourg, a corps of 700 men armed with this weapon were considered to be the flower of the English infantry.

To trace the true origin of the longbow is not easy. There are reasons for believing that it may have been borrowed from the South Welsh, who were certainly provided with it as early as A.D. 1150.[2] Against this derivation, however, may be pleaded the fact that in the first half of the thirteenth century it appears to have been in greater vogue in the northern than in the western counties of England. As a national weapon it is first accepted in the Assize of Arms of 1252, wherein all holders of 40s. in land or nine marks in chattels are desired to provide themselves with sword, dagger, bow, and arrows.[3] Contemporary documents often speak of the obligation of various manors to provide the king with one or more archers "when he makes an expedition against the Welsh." It is curious to observe that even as late as 1281 the preference for the crossbow seems to have been kept up, the wages of its bearer being considerably more than those of the archer.[4]

To Edward I the longbow owes its original rise into favor. That monarch, like his grandson and great-grandson, was an able soldier, capable of devising new expedients in war. Unlike them, he also showed considerable strategical ability. His long experience in Welsh campaigns led him to introduce a scientific use of archery much like that which William the Conqueror had employed at Hastings. We are informed that it was first put into practice in a combat fought against Prince Llewelyn at Orwin Bridge (A.D.

[2] Gerald de Barri speaks of the Welsh bowmen as being able to send an arrow through an oak door four fingers thick. The people of Gwent (Monmouth and Glamorgan) were reckoned the best archers. Those of North Wales were always spearmen, not archers. *Giraldus Cambrensis Itinerarium Kambriae*, ed. James F. Dimock (Rolls Series; London, 1868), p. 54.

[3] William Stubbs, *Select Charters* (9th ed.; Oxford, 1913), p. 364.

[4] In the Pay Roll of the garrison of Rhuddlan castle, 1281, we find "paid to Geoffrey le Chamberlin for the wages of twelve crossbowmen, and thirteen archers, for twenty-four days, £7 8s., each cross-bowman receiving by the day 4d., and each archer 2d."

1282), and afterwards copied by the Earl of Warwick in another engagement fought near Conway during the year 1295.

The Welsh, on the earl's approach, set themselves fronting his force with exceeding long spears, which, being suddenly turned toward the earl and his company, with their ends placed in the earth and their points upward, broke the force of the English cavalry. But the earl well provided against them, by placing archers between his men-at-arms, so that by these missive weapons those who held the lances were put to rout.[5]

The battle of Falkirk (A.D. 1298), however, was the first engagement of real importance in which the bowmen, properly supplemented by cavalry, played the leading part. Its circumstances, indeed, bore such striking witness to the power of the arrow that it could not fail to serve as a lesson to English commanders. The Scots of the Lowlands, who formed the army of William Wallace, consisted mainly of spearmen, armed, like the Swiss, with a pike many feet in length. They had in their ranks a small body of horse, a few hundred in number, and a certain proportion of archers, mainly drawn from the Ettrick and Selkirk district. Wallace, having selected an excellent position behind a marsh, formed his spearmen in four great masses (or *schiltrons*, as the Scotch called them) of circular form, ready to face outward in any direction. The light troops formed a line in the intervals of these columns, while the cavalry were placed in reserve. Edward came on with his horsemen in three divisions; his archers were disposed between them. The foremost English "battle," that of the Earl Marshal, rode

[5] Nicholas Trivet, *Annales,* ed. Thomas Hog (London, 1845), pp. 335–336.

into the morass, was stopped by it, and suffered severely from the Scotch missile weapons. The second division, commanded by the bishop of Durham, observing this check, rode around the flank of the marsh in order to turn Wallace's position. At the approach of the English knights the small body of Scotch cavalry turned and rode off the field without striking a blow. Then the bishop's horsemen charged the hostile line from the rear. The squadrons opposed to the light troops succeeded in riding them down, as Wallace's archers were only armed with the short bow and were not particularly skilled in its use. Those of the English, however, who faced the masses of pikemen received a sanguinary check, and were thrown back in disorder. The bishop had therefore to await the arrival of the king, who was leading the infantry and the remainder of the cavalry around the end of the marsh.

When this had been done, Edward brought up his bowmen close to the Scotch masses, who were unable to reply (as their own light troops had been driven away) or to charge, on account of the nearness of the English men-at-arms. Concentrating the rain of arrows on particular points in the columns, the king fairly riddled the Scotch ranks, and then sent in his cavalry with a sudden charge. The plan succeeded; the shaken parts of the masses were pierced, and the knights, having once got within the pikes, made a fearful slaughter of the enemy. The moral of the fight was evident: cavalry could not beat the Scotch tactics, but archers supplemented by horsemen could easily accomplish the required task.

Accordingly, for the next two centuries the characteristics of the fight of Falkirk were continually repeated whenever the English and the Scotch met. Halidon Hill (A.D.

1333), Neville's Cross (A.D. 1346), Homildon (A.D. 1402), and Flodden (A.D. 1513) were all variations on the same theme. The steady but slow-moving masses of the Lowland infantry fell a sacrifice to their own persistent bravery when they staggered on in a vain endeavor to reach the line of men-at-arms, flanked by archers, whom the English commander opposed to them. The bowman might boast with truth that he "carried twelve Scots' lives at his girdle"; he had but to launch his shaft into the easy target of the great surging mass of pikemen, and it was sure to do execution.

[Bannockburn (A.D. 1314), indeed, forms a notable exception to the general rule. Its result, however, was not due to an attempt to discard the tactics of Falkirk, but to unskillful, almost insane generalship, which one might have expected of a campaign conducted by Edward II. The forces of Robert Bruce, much like those of Wallace in composition, may have amounted to 10,000 men and 500 picked horsemen. Bruce had taken up a strong position in the New Park, covering the town and castle of Stirling, which Edward had sworn to relieve. The Scottish king had made his dispositions to meet an attack along the old Roman road which ran from Falkirk to Stirling, but the English, who had made a strong reconnaissance on the afternoon of June 23, 1314, decided to try and turn the Scots' position under cover of darkness. They spent, therefore, the night of June 23–24 in crossing the Bannockburn between Bannockburn village and Crookbridge, an area which in the fourteenth century was extremely wet. Edward's army, numbering close to 20,000 men, spent all night in passing the stream, and dawn found them still a disorganized mass milling about on the flats below St. Ninian's church. Only the vanguard under the Earl of Gloucester had managed to

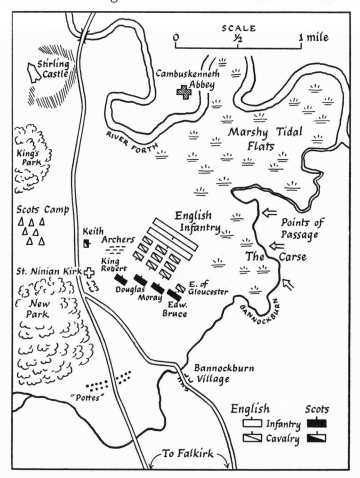

Fig. 4. Military plan of the battle of Bannockburn, 1314.

get into some sort of order. This presented Bruce with a golden opportunity which he hastened to use. Facing his army to the new front, he launched them down the slope in echelon of *schiltrons* strikingly like the normal Swiss order of attack, and crashed into the weltering mass of English with devastating effect. A few of the English archers had got into position on their own right flank, but these were ridden down and chased off the field by a charge of the Scottish cavalry under the marshal Keith, the single noteworthy deed ever recorded of the Scottish knighthood.

[The battle developed into a confused melee between the spearmen of Bruce and Edward's knights. The latter, cramped for room, could make only partial and ineffective charges which failed utterly to break the lines of pikes. Meanwhile they suffered frightful casualties. The rear ranks could not get up to join the combat and stood helpless while their comrades were mowed down. Finally, either through exhaustion or through a Scottish stratagem, the entire English front broke to pieces, and the defeat became a rout. Behind them lay the marshy banks of the Bannockburn and the broad reaches of the river Forth. Hundreds were drowned in attempting to escape. King Edward himself eluded capture by taking a circuitous route which led him past Stirling castle, where the governor refused him admittance. Never before or since has such a dreadful slaughter of the English baronage taken place, nor has such a defeat been administered to an English army. Its lessons were obvious. Cavalry, no matter how brave or how determined, cannot defeat steady pikemen unaided, and archers unsupported by heavy troops are worthless.][6]

The next series of campaigns in which the English bowman was to take part were directed against an enemy

[6] These paragraphs have been rewritten by the editor for this edition. They are based in part on John Barbour, *The Bruce,* tr. Geo. Eyre-Todd (Glasgow, 1907), pp. 222–223, W. M. MacKenzie, *The Battle of Bannockburn* (Glasgow, 1913), and John E. Morris, *Bannockburn* (Cambridge, 1914).

different in every respect from the sturdy spearman of the Lowlands. In France those absurd perversions of the art of war which covered themselves under the name of chivalry were more omnipotent than in any other country of Europe. The strength of the armies of Philip and John of Valois was composed of a fiery and undisciplined aristocracy which imagined itself to be the most efficient military force in the world, but which was in reality little removed from an armed mob. A system which reproduced on the battlefield the distinctions of feudal society was considered by the French noble to represent the ideal form of warlike organization. He firmly believed that, since he was infinitely superior to any peasant in the social scale, he must consequently excel the peasant to the same extent in military value. He was, therefore, prone not only to despise all descriptions of infantry but to regard their appearance on the field against him as a species of insult to his class pride. The self-confidence of the French nobility—shaken for the moment by the result of Courtrai—had reasserted itself after the bloody days of Mons-en-Pévèle and Cassel. The fate which had on those occasions befallen the gallant but ill-trained burghers of Flanders was believed to be only typical of that which awaited any foot soldier who dared to match himself against the chivalry of the most warlike aristocracy in Christendom. Pride goes before a fall, and the French noble was now to meet infantry of a quality such as he had never supposed to exist.

Against these presumptuous cavaliers, their mercenaries, and the wretched band of half-armed villeins whom they dragged with them to the battlefield, the English archer was now matched. He was by this time almost a professional soldier, being usually not a pressed man, but a volunteer, raised by one of those barons or knights with whom the king contracted for a supply of soldiers. Led to enlist by sheer love of fighting, desire for adventures, or hope of plunder, he possessed a great moral ascendancy over the spiritless hordes who followed the French nobility to the wars. Historians, however, have laid too much stress on this superiority, real as it was. No amount of mere readiness to fight would have accounted for the English victories of the fourteenth century. Self-confidence and pugnacity were not wanting in the Fleming at Roosebeke or the Scot at Falkirk, yet they did not secure success. It was the excellent armament and tactics of the yeomanry, even more than their courage, which made them masters of the field at Crécy or Poitiers.

The longbow had as yet been employed only in offensive warfare, and against an enemy inferior in cavalry to the English army. When, however, Edward III led his invading force into France, the conditions of war were entirely changed. The French were invariably superior in the numbers of their horsemen, and the tactics of the archer had to be adapted to the defensive. He was soon to find that the charging squadron presented as good a mark for his shaft as the stationary column of infantry. Nothing indeed could be more disconcerting to a body of cavalry than a flight of arrows: not only did it lay low a certain proportion of the riders, but it caused such disorder by setting the wounded horses plunging and rearing among their fellows that it was most effective in checking the impetus of the onset. As the distance grew shorter and the range more easy, the wounds to horse and man became more numerous; the disorder increased, the pace continued to slacken, and at last a limit was reached beyond which the squadron could not pass. To force a line of longbowmen by a mere front attack was a task almost hopeless for cavalry. This, however, was a fact which the continental world had yet to learn in the year 1346.

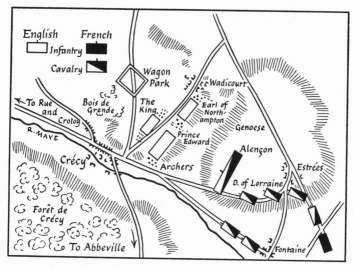

Fig. 5. Military plan of the battle of Crécy, 1346.

[At Crécy (A.D. 1346) King Edward III divided his army of approximately 11,000 men into the usual three "battles." The right wing was commanded by the Prince of Wales and occupied the hillside halfway between the river Maye and the village of Wadicourt. It consisted of 800 dismounted men-at-arms flanked on either side by archers, 2,000 all told, and about 1,000 Welsh spearmen. On the prince's left and somewhat drawn back lay the second corps under the joint command of the earls of Arundel and Northampton. It was somewhat smaller than the first, consisting of about 500 men-at-arms and 1,200 archers, arrayed in the same manner. Its right rested on the prince's left, and its left flank was protected by the village of Wadicourt. King Edward himself, with the reserve of 700 men-at-arms, 2,000 archers, and perhaps 1,000 Welsh spearmen, lay on the plateau in front of the wood of La Grange, behind the "battle" of the Prince of Wales.] [7]

Nothing could be more characteristic of the indiscipline of the French army than the fact that it forced the battle a day sooner than its leader had intended. On observing the English position, Philip and his marshals had determined to defer the conflict till the next morning, as the troops had been marching since daybreak. When, however, the order to halt reached the vanguard, the nobles at the head of the column believed that they were to be deprived of the honor of opening the fight, as they could see that some of the troops in the rear were still advancing. They therefore pushed on, and, as the main body persisted in following them, the whole army arrived so close to the English position that a battle became unavoidable. The circumstances of that day have often been described; it is unnecessary to detail the mishap of the unfortunate Genoese crossbowmen, who were shot down in scores while going through the cumbrous process of winding up their arbalests. The fruitless charges of the cavalry against the front of the line of archers led to endless slaughter, till the ground was heaped with the bodies of men and horses, and further attempts to advance became impossible.

[The main assault of the French seems always to have been directed against the dismounted men-at-arms, rather than against the archers, and sometimes pressed them

[7] This paragraph has been rewritten by the editor.

severely, but in no instance did the English line yield a single foot. The knights fell before the line of lances, which they were unable to break, and fared no better than their comrades in the center. At nightfall the French fell back in disorder, and their whole army dispersed. The English had won the day without stirring a foot from their position; the enemy had come to them to be killed.] Considerably more than a third of his numbers lay dead in front of the English line, and of these far the greatest number had fallen by the arrows of the bowmen.

Crécy had proved that the archer, when adequately supported by dismounted men-at-arms, could beat off the most determined charges of cavalry. The moral, however, which was drawn from it by the French was one of a different kind. Unwilling, in the bitterness of their class pride, to ascribe the victory to the arms of mere peasants, they came to the conclusion that it was due to the stability of the phalanx of dismounted knights.

Bearing this in mind, King John, at the battle of Poitiers (A.D. 1356), resolved to imitate the successful expedient of King Edward. He commanded the whole of his cavalry, with the exception of two small corps—a forlorn hope—to shorten their spears, take off their spurs, and send their horses to the rear. He had failed to observe that the circumstances of attack and of defense are absolutely different. Troops who intend to root themselves to a given spot of ground adopt tactics the very opposite of those required for an assault on a strong position. The device which was well chosen for the protection of Edward's flanks at Crécy was ludicrous when adopted as a means for storming the hill of Maupertuis. Vigorous impact, not stability, was the quality at which the king should have

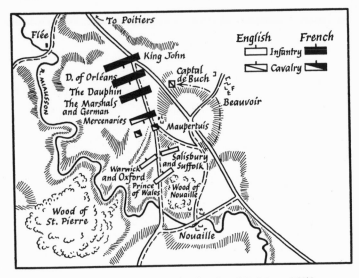

Fig. 6. Military plan of the battle of Poitiers, 1356.

aimed. Nothing, indeed, could have been more fatal than
John's conduct throughout the day. The battle itself was
most unnecessary, since the Black Prince could have been
starved into surrender in less than a week. [In fact, the
position of the English was so desperate that on the morning of the battle, Prince Edward attempted to withdraw
without fighting, and accepted the decision of arms only
when the French engaged his rear guard in force.] If, however, fighting was to take place, it was absolutely insane to
form the whole French army into a gigantic wedge—where
corps after corps was massed behind the first and narrowest
line—and to dash it against the strongest point of the English front. This, however, was the plan which the king
determined to adopt. Access to the plateau of Maupertuis
lay over a terrain covered by bushes and trees, and was

protected by a hedge along which the English archers were posted. Through a gap in the hedge John thrust his vanguard, a chosen body of 300 horsemen, while the rest of his forces, three great masses of dismounted cavalry, followed close behind.

It is needless to say that the archers shot down the greater part of the advanced corps and sent the survivors reeling back against the first "battle" in their rear. This at once fell into disorder, which was largely increased when the archers proceeded to concentrate their attention on its ranks. Before a blow had been struck at close quarters, the French were growing demoralized under the shower of arrows. Seeing his opportunity, the Prince at once came down from the plateau and fell on the front of the shaken column with all his men-at-arms. At the same moment a small ambuscade of 60 men-at-arms and 100 archers which he had dispatched under the Captal de Buch to create a diversion appeared on the French left flank. This was too much for King John's men; without waiting for further attacks about two-thirds of them left the field. A corps of Germans in the second "battle" and the troops immediately around the monarch's person were the only portions of the army which made a creditable resistance. The English, however, were able to surround these bodies at their leisure, and ply bow and lance alternately against them till they broke up. Then John, his son Philip, and such of his nobles as had remained with him were forced to surrender.

This was a splendid tactical triumph for the prince, who secured the victory by the excellence of the position he had chosen and by the judicious use made of his archery. John's new device for attacking an English army had failed, with far greater ignominy than had attended the rout of his predecessor's feudal chivalry at Crécy. So greatly did the result of the day of Poitiers affect the French mind that no further attempt was made to meet the invader in a pitched battle during the continuance of the war. Confounded at the blow which had been delivered against their old military system, the noblesse of France foreswore the open field and sullenly shut themselves up in their castles, resolved to confine their operations to petty sieges and incursions. The English might march through the length and breadth of the land—as did the Earl of Lancaster in 1373—but they could no longer draw their opponents out to fight. Entrenched behind walls which the invader had no leisure to attack, the French allowed him to waste his strength in toilsome marches through a deserted country. Opposed as was this form of war to all the precepts of chivalry—which bid the good knight to accept every challenge—they were on the whole well suited to the exigencies of the time. The tactics of Charles V and Du Guesclin won back all that those of King John had lost. The English found that the war was no longer a means of displaying great feats of arms, but a monotonous and inglorious occupation which involved a constant drain of blood and money and no longer maintained itself from the resources of the enemy.

Common sense, and not aphorisms drawn from the customs of the tournament, guided the campaigns of Du Guesclin. He took the field not in the spirit of adventure but in the spirit of business. His end being to edge and worry the English out of France, he did not care whether that consummation was accomplished by showy exploits or by unobtrusive hard work. He would fight, if necessary, but was just as ready to reach his goal by craft as by hard blows. Night surprises, ambuscades, and stratagems of every description were his choice, in preference to open attacks. Provided with a continual supply of men by his free companies, he was never obliged to hazard an engagement for fear that his forces might melt away without having done any service. This relieved him from that necessity to hurry operations which had been fatal to so many generals commanding the temporary hosts of feudalism. The English were better fitted for winning great battles than for carrying on a series of harassing campaigns. Tactics, not strategy, were their forte, and a succession of petty sieges and inglorious retreats put an end to their ill-judged attempt to hold by force a foreign dominion beyond the Channel.

Du Guesclin, however, had only cleared the way for the reappearance of the French noblesse on the field. Shut up in their castles while the free companies were reconquering the country, they had apparently "forgotten nothing and remembered nothing." With the fear of the English no longer before their eyes, they at once reverted to their old chivalrous practices. The last years of the century were similar to the first: if Cassel reproduced itself at Roosebeke, a nemesis awaited the revived tactics of feudalism, and Nicopolis was a more disastrous edition of Courtrai. Thirty years of anarchy, during the reign of an imbecile king, fostered the reactionary and unscientific tendency of the wars of the time and made France a fit prey to a new series of English invasions.

If subsequent campaigns had not proved that Henry V was a master of strategical combinations, we should be inclined to pronounce his march to Agincourt a rash and unjustifiable undertaking. It is, however, probable that he had taken the measure of his enemies and gauged their imbecility before he sacrificed his communications and threw himself into Picardy. The rapidity of his movements from October 6–24, 1415,[8] shows that he had that appreciation of the value of time which was so rare among mediaeval commanders, while the perfect organization of his columns on the march proved that his genius could condescend to details.[9] Near St. Pol-sur-Tenoise the French barred Henry's further progress with a great feudal army three or four times larger than that of the English. Like the two Edwards at Crécy and Poitiers, the king resolved to fight a defensive battle, in spite of the scantiness of his force. He had with him not more than 6,000 men, of whom approximately 5,000 were archers. The position chosen by Henry was as excellent in its way as could be desired; it had a frontage of not more than twelve hundred yards, and was covered by woods on either flank. The land over which the enemy would have to advance consisted of ploughed fields, thoroughly sodden by a week of rain. [King Henry drew up the English line on the old plan of Crécy and Auray, with the usual three "battles" of dismounted men-at-arms, each flanked by slightly projecting wings of archers. The king commanded the center; Edward, Duke of York, the right wing, and Lord Camoys the left. The archers protected their front with rows of sharpened stakes pointing toward the enemy.

[The constable of France, though nominally in command, was so harassed by the presence of numerous royal counts and dukes in his army that he really cannot be held responsible for the conduct of the battle. The French, obsessed with the idea that some strange virtue was attached

[8] He went 320 miles in eighteen days.

[9] See for Henry's columns of route the *Gesta Henrici Quinti*, ed. Benjamin Williams (London, 1850), pp. 37–46.

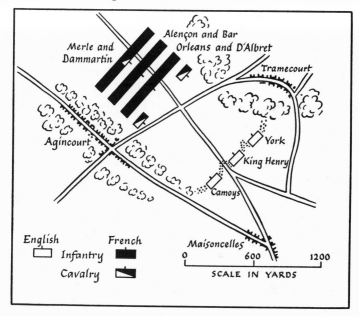

Fig. 7. Military plan of the battle of Agincourt, 1415.

to the practice of dismounting cavalry, exactly repeated the example set by King John at Poitiers, and the bulk of the men-at-arms were directed to send their horses to the rear. The army was drawn up into three "battles," one behind the other and preceded by two small squadrons of mounted men. The third "battle" also retained its horses for use in the pursuit. The French had brought a relatively small number of infantry, chiefly crossbowmen, to the field, and these were stationed in the rear of each "battle," where they could be of no possible use.

[King Henry remained in his prepared position for some time, awaiting the enemy, for he well knew that his only chance for victory lay in provoking the French to attack.

Finally he ordered his little army to move forward until it was within long archery range of the first French line. This produced the desired result. The two squadrons of cavalry began to move, and the line of dismounted men-at-arms began to push forward through the mud. The English archers refixed their stakes and prepared to meet the attack. The cavalry were mostly shot down before they reached the line of stakes, and those who did reach the stakes were quickly disposed of at point-blank range. Meanwhile the French troops of the first line were lurching heavily across almost a mile of water-logged ground, sinking to their ankles in the mud, while all the time the English arrows played upon them, taking a heavy toll. Nonetheless, the English line was shaken at the first impact of the heavily armored formation, and it was re-established only by the fiercest hand-to-hand fighting. The decisive moment came when King Henry ordered his archers to put aside their bows and fall to with ax and sword. Exhausted by the combat and by their long struggle through the mud, the French men-at-arms were no match for their lighter-armed opponents. Helplessly they stood while the agile yeomen "beat upon their armor with mallets, as though they were smiths hammering upon anvils." The first French line was thrown back in disorder upon the second "battle" as it came up to join the action. The English reformed their line and advanced to meet the new threat. The struggle was not long, for the newcomers were shaken and demoralized before they ever struck a blow. Soon the second line broke and made for the rear, while the third division melted away without even making a charge.] [10]

Few commanders could have committed a more glaring

[10] This paragraph has been rewritten by the editor.

series of blunders than did the constable, but the chief fault of his design lay in attempting to attack an English army, established in a good position, at all. [The time had come when defensive armor had become so heavy that its wearer, once he had become exhausted, was at the mercy of a light-armed yeoman.] The true course here, as at Poitiers, would have been to have starved the king, who was living merely on the resources of the neighborhood, out of his position. If, however, an attack was projected, it should have been accompanied by a turning movement around the woods, and preceded by the use of all the arbalesters and archers of the army, a force which we know to have been far superior to that of the English in point of numbers.

Such a day as Agincourt might have been expected to break the French noblesse of its love for an obsolete system of tactics. So intimately, however, was the feudal array bound up with the feudal scheme of society that it yet remained the ideal order of battle. Three bloody defeats—Cravant (A.D. 1423), Verneuil (A.D. 1424), and the Day of the Herrings (A.D. 1429)—were the consequences of a fanatical adherence to the old method of fighting. On each of those occasions the French columns, sometimes composed of horsemen and sometimes of dismounted knights, made a desperate attempt to break an English array of archers by a front attack, and on each occasion they were driven back in utter rout.

It was not till the conduct of the war fell into the hands of professional soldiers like Xaintrailles, La Hire, and Dunois that these insane tactics were discarded. Their abandonment, however, was only the first step toward success for the French. The position of the country was infinitely worse than it had been in the days of Du Guesclin,

since the greater part of the districts north of the Loire were
not only occupied by the English but had resigned themselves to their fate, and showed no desire to join the national party. A petty warfare such as had won back the
lands of Aquitaine from the Black Prince would have been
totally inadequate to rescue France in 1428. It is on this
ground that we must base the importance of the influence
of the Maid of Orleans. Her successes represent, not a
new tactical system, but the awakening of a popular enthusiasm which was to make the further stay of the English
in France impossible. The smaller country could not hold
down the larger unless the population of the latter were
supine; when they ceased to be so, the undertaking—in
spite of all military superiority—became impossible.

While ascribing the expulsion of the English from France
to political rather than strategical reasons, we must not
forget that the professional officers of the fifteenth century
had at last discovered a method of minimizing the ascendancy of the English soldiery. When they found the invaders
drawn up in a good defensive position, they invariably refrained from attacking them. There was no object in making
the troops a target to be riddled with arrows, when success
was almost impossible. Accordingly, the French victories
of the second quarter of the century will be found to have
resulted in most cases from attacking an English army at
a moment when it was on the march or in some other position which rendered it impossible for an order of battle to
be rapidly formed. Patay (A.D. 1429) is a fair example of
a conflict of this description; the battle was lost because
Talbot when attacked was not immediately ready. Expecting to see the whole French army arrive on the field and
draw itself up in battle array, he paid no attention to the

mere vanguard which was before him, and commenced falling back on the village of Patay, where he intended to form his line. La Hire, however, without waiting for the main body to come up, attacked the retreating columns and forced his way among them "before the archers had time to fix their stakes." [11] The superiority of the bow to the lance depended on the ability of the bearer of the missile weapon to keep his enemy at a distance. If once, by any accident, the cavalry got among their opponents, a mere melee ensued, and numbers and weight carried the day. Such was the case on this occasion; La Hire having succeeded in closing, the battle resolved itself into a hand-to-hand struggle, and when the main body of the French came up, the English were overpowered by numerical superiority. Such were the usual tactical causes of English defeats in the fifteenth century.

The fall of the empire which Henry V had established in France was therefore due, from the military point of view, to the inadequacy of a purely defensive system to meet all the vicissitudes of a series of campaigns. The commanders who had received the tradition of Agincourt and Poitiers disliked assuming the offensive. Accustomed to win success by receiving the enemy's attack on a carefully chosen ground, and after deliberate preparations, they frequently failed when opposed to officers who refrained on principle from assailing a position, but were continually appearing when least expected. In the open field or on the march, in camp or the town, the English were always liable to a sudden onslaught. They were too good as soldiers to

[11] C. W. C. Oman, *The History of England from the Accession of Richard II to the Death of Richard III (1377–1485)*, (Hunt-Poole Series; London, 1920), pp. 308–309; Lot, *op. cit.*, II, 55.

be demoralized, but they lost the old confidence which had distinguished them in the days when the French still persisted in keeping up their ancient feudal tactics.

A fortunate chance has preserved for us, in the pages of Blondel's *Reductio Normanniae,* a full account of the disastrous field of Formigny, April 15, 1450, the last battle but one fought by the English in their attempt to hold down their dominion beyond the Channel. The narrative is most instructive as explaining the changes of fortune during the later years of the great war. The fight itself—though destined to decide the fate of all Normandy—was an engagement on a very small scale. Some 4,500 English, half of them archers, the remainder billmen for the most part, with a few hundred men-at-arms, had been collected for a desperate attempt to open the way to Caen. In that town the Duke of Somerset, commander of all the English armies in France, was threatened by an overwhelming host led by King Charles in person. To draw together a force capable of taking the field, all the Norman fortresses had been stripped of their garrisons, and such reinforcements as could be procured, some 2,500 men at most, had been brought across from England. The relieving army succeeded in taking Valognes and forcing the dangerous fords of the Douve and Vire, but hard by the village of Formigny it was confronted by a French corps under the Count of Clermont, one of several divisions which had been sent out to arrest the march of the English. Clermont's troops did not greatly exceed their enemies in number: they appear, as far as conflicting accounts allow us to judge, to have consisted of 600 *lances garnis* (i.e., 3,000 combatants), two small pieces of artillery, and some local infantry.

The obligation to take the offensive rested with the English, who were bound to force their way to Caen. Nevertheless, Sir Thomas Kyriel and Sir Matthew Gough, the two veterans who commanded the relieving army, refused to assume the initiative. The old prejudice in favor of fighting defensive battles was so strong that, forgetting the object of their expedition, they fell back and looked for a position in which to receive the attack of Clermont's troops. Finding a brook lined with orchards and plantations, which was well calculated to cover their rear, they halted in front of it and drew up their men in a convex line, the center projecting, the wings drawn back so as to touch the stream. Three bodies of archers—each 700 strong—formed the "main battle"; on the flanks of this force were stationed two "battles" of billmen, not in a line with the center but drawn back from it, while these corps were themselves flanked by the small force of cavalry, which was formed close in front of the orchards and the brook. Clermont did not attack immediately, so that the archers had ample time to fix their stakes, according to their invariable custom, and the whole force was beginning to cover itself with a trench [12] when the enemy at last began to move. Through long experience the French had grown too wary to attack an English line of archers from the front; after feeling the position, they tried several partial assaults on the flanks, which were repulsed. Skirmishing had been going on for three hours without any decisive result when Giraud, master of the royal ordinance, brought up the two culverins and placed

---

[12] *Gladio ad usum fossarum verso, et ungue verrente tellurem concavant: et ante se campum equis inadibilem mira hostium astucia efficiebat* (Gilles Le Bouvier, Berry Herald, *Le Recouvrement de Normandie*, ed. Joseph Stevenson, in *Narratives of the Expulsion of the English from Normandy* [Rolls Series; London, 1863], p. 333).

them in a spot from which they enfiladed the English line. Galled by the fire of these pieces, part of the archers rushed out from behind their stakes and with the aid of one of the wings of billmen charged the French, seized the culverins, and routed the troops which protected them.

If the whole of Kyriel's force had advanced at this moment, the battle might have been won.[13] But the English commander adhered rigidly to his defensive tactics, and while he waited motionless, the fate of the battle was changed. The troops who had charged were attacked by one of the flank "battles" of French men-at-arms, who had dismounted and advanced to win back the lost cannon; a desperate fight took place, while the English strove to drag the pieces toward their lines and the enemy tried to recapture them. At last the French prevailed, and pushing the retreating body before them reached the English position. The archers were unable to use their arrows, so closely were friend and foe intermixed in the crowd of combatants which slowly rolled back toward them. Thus the two armies met all along the line in a hand-to-hand combat, and a sanguinary melee began. The fate of the battle was still doubtful when a new French force arrived in the field. The counts of Richemont and Laval, coming up from Saint-Lô, appeared on the rear of the English position with 1,200 men-at-arms. All Kyriel's troops were engaged, and he was unable to meet this new attack. His men recoiled to the brook at their backs, and were at once broken into several isolated corps. Gough cut his way through the French, and reached Bayeux with the cavalry. But Kyriel and the infantry were surrounded, and the whole main "battle" was annihilated. A few hundred archers escaped, and their

[13] Lot, *op. cit.*, II, 82.

commander, with some scores more, was taken prisoner, but the French gave little quarter,[14] and their heralds counted next day about 4,000 English corpses lying on the field. Seldom has an army suffered such a complete disaster: of Kyriel's small force not less than four-fifths was destroyed. What number of the French fell we are unable to ascertain; their annalists speak of the death of twelve knights, none of them men of note, but make no further mention of their losses. An English chronicler observes sarcastically:

They declare what number they slew, but they write not how many of themselves were slain and destroyed. This was well nigh the first foughten field they gat on the English, wherefore I blame them not; though they of a little make much, and set forth all, and hide nothing that may sound to their glory.[15]

The moral of Formigny was evident: an unintelligent application of the defensive tactics of Edward III and Henry V could lead only to disaster when the French had improved in military skill and were no longer accustomed to make gross blunders at every engagement. Unless some new method of dealing with the superior numbers and cautious maneuvers of the disciplined *compagnies d'ordonnance* of Charles VII could be devised, the English were foredoomed by their numerical inferiority to defeat. It was probably a perception of this fact which induced the great Talbot to discard his old tactics and employ at his last fight a method of attack totally unlike that practiced in the rest of the Hundred Years' War. The accounts of the battle of Castillon (A.D. 1453) recall the warfare of the

[14] Richard Grafton, *Chronicle; or History of England* (London, 1809), I, 635.
[15] *Ibid.*

Swiss rather than of the English armies. That engagement was a desperate attempt of a column of dismounted men-at-arms and billmen, flanked by archers, to storm an entrenched camp protected by artillery. The English—like the Swiss at La Bicocca—found the task too hard for them, and only increased the disaster by their gallant persistence in attempting to accomplish the impossible.

The expulsion of the English from their continental possessions had no permanent effect in discrediting the power of the bow. The weapon still retained its supremacy as a missile weapon over the clumsy arbalest with its complicated array of wheels and levers. It was hardly less superior to the newly invented handguns and arquebuses, which did not attain any great degree of efficiency before the end of the century. The testimony of all Europe was given in favor of the longbow. Charles of Burgundy considered a corps of 3,000 English bowmen the flower of his infantry. Charles of France, 30 years earlier, had made the archer the basis of his new militia in a vain attempt to naturalize the weapon of his enemies beyond the Channel. James of Scotland, after a similar endeavor, had resigned himself to ill success, and turned the archery of his subjects to ridicule.

There are few periods which appear more likely to present to the inquirer a series of interesting military problems than the years of the great struggle in which the national weapons and national tactics of the English were turned against each other. The Wars of the Roses were, however, unfortunate in their historians. The dearth of exact information concerning the various engagements is remarkable when we consider the ample materials which are to be found for the history of the preceding periods. The meager annals of William of Worcester, Warkworth,

Fabyan, of the continuer of the *Croyland Chronicle*, and the author of the *Arrival of King Edward IV*, with the ignorant generalities of Whethamstede, are insufficiently supplemented by the later works of Grafton and Hall. When all has been collated, we still fail to grasp the details of most of the battles. Not in one single instance can we reconstruct the exact array of a Yorkist or a Lancastrian army. Enough, however, survives to make us regret the scantiness of the sources of our information.

That some considerable amount of tactical and strategical skill was employed by many of the English commanders is evident when we analyze the general characteristics of their campaigns. The engagements show no stereotyped similarity of incident such as would have resulted from a general adherence to a single form of attack or defense. Each combat had its own individuality, resulting from the particular tactics employed in it. The fierce street fight which is known as the first battle of St. Albans (A.D. 1455) has nothing in common with the irregular skirmishing of Hedgeley Moor (A.D. 1464). The stormings of the fortified positions of Northampton (A.D. 1460) and Tewkesbury (A.D. 1471) bear no resemblance to the pitched battles of Towton (A.D. 1461) and Barnet (A.D. 1471). The superiority of tactics which won Blore Heath (A.D. 1459) contrasts with the superiority of armament which won Edgecott Field (A.D. 1469).

Prominent among the features of the war stands out the generalship of King Edward IV. Already a skillful commander in his nineteenth year, it was he who at Northampton turned the Lancastrian position by forcing the "streight places" which covered the flank of the line of high banks and deep trenches behind which the army of King Henry was sheltered.[16] A year later (1461) he saved a cause which seemed desperate by his rapid march from Gloucester to London, a march executed in the inclement month of February and over the miry roads of the south Midland counties. The decision of mind which led him to attempt at all hazards to throw himself into the capital won him his crown and turned the balance at the decisive crisis of the war. If, when settled on the throne, he imperiled his position by carelessness and presumption, he was himself again at the first blast of the trumpet. His vigorous struggle in the spring of 1470, when all around him were showing themselves traitors, was a wonderful example of the success of prompt action.[17] Nor was his genius less marked in his last great military success, the campaign of Barnet and Tewkesbury.

To have marched from York to London, threading his way among the hosts of his foes without disaster, was a skillful achievement, even if the treachery of some of the hostile commanders is taken into consideration. At Barnet he showed that tactics no less than strategy lay within the compass of his powers, by turning the casual circumstance of the fog entirely to his own profit. The unforeseen chance by which each army outflanked the other was not in itself more favorable to one party than to the other; it merely tested the relative ability of the two leaders. But Edward's care in providing a reserve rendered the defeat of his left wing unimportant, while the similar disaster on Warwick's

[16] Edward Hall, *Chronicle; containing the History of England* (London, 1809), p. 244.

[17] The whole country being disaffected and ready—as the events of the autumn proved—to revolt in favor of Warwick or Henry VI, the suppression of the Lincolnshire rebellion and the expulsion of the kingmaker were remarkable achievements.

left was turned to such good account that it decided the day. Warwick himself, indeed, if we investigate his whole career, leaves on us the impression rather of the political wirepuller, *le plus subtil homme de son vivant,* as Commynes called him, than of the great military figure of traditional accounts.

Barnet being won, the second half of the campaign began with Edward's march to intercept Queen Margaret before she could open communications with her friends in South Wales. Gloucester was held for the king; his enemies, therefore, as they marched north, were compelled to make for Tewkesbury, the first crossing on the Severn which was passable for them. The Lancastrian feint on Chipping Sodbury was not ill-judged, but Edward rendered its effect nugatory by his rapid movements. Both armies gathered themselves up for a rush toward the all-important passage, but the king—although he had the longer distance to cover, and was toiling over the barren, rolling country of the Cotswold Plateau—outmarched his opponents. Men spoke with surprise of the thirty-two miles which his army accomplished in the day, without halting for a meal, and in a district where water was so scarce that the men were able to quench their thirst only once in the twelve hours.[18] By evening the king was within five miles of the Lancastrians, who had halted, utterly worn out, in the town of Tewkesbury. As they had not succeeded in crossing its ferry that night, they were compelled to fight the next day, since there was even greater danger in being attacked while their forces were half across the Severn and half still on the Gloucestershire side than in turning to meet the king.

[18] This must have been in the Stroudwater, as Edward marched from Wooton-under-Edge by Stroud and Painswick on Cheltenham.

Queen Margaret's generals therefore drew up their forces on the rising ground to the south of the town, in a good position where they had the slope of the hill in their favor and were well protected by hedges and high banks. Edward, however, made no rash attempts to force his enemies' line; instead of delivering an assault he brought up cannon and archers and concentrated their fire on one of the hostile wings. Somerset, who commanded there, was at last so galled that he came down from his vantage ground to drive off the gunners. His charge was for the moment successful, but left a fatal gap in the Lancastrian line. The center making no attempt to close this opening,[19] Edward was enabled to thrust his main "battle" into it, and thus forced the position and drove his enemies in complete disorder into the cul-de-sac of Tewkesbury town, where they were for the most part compelled to surrender. It will at once be observed that the king's tactics on this occasion were precisely those which had won for William the Norman the field of Hastings. He repeated the experiment, combining artillery with archery, and put his enemy in a position where he had either to fall back or to charge in order to escape the Yorkist missiles.

King Edward was by no means the only commander of merit whom the war revealed. We should be inclined to rate the Earl of Salisbury's ability high, after considering his maneuver at Blore Heath. Being at the head of inferior forces, he retired for some time before Lord Audley till,

[19] Somerset attributed this to treachery on the part of Lord Wenlock, commander of the center "battle," who was a follower of Warwick and not an old Lancastrian. Escaping from the advancing Yorkists, Somerset rode up to Wenlock and, after cursing him for a traitor, brained him with his battle-ax (Hall, *op. cit.*, p. 300).

continued retreat having made his adversary careless, he suddenly turned on him while his forces were divided by a stream, and inflicted crushing blows on the two isolated halves of the Lancastrian army. The operations before Towton also seem to show the existence of considerable enterprise and alertness on both sides. Clifford was successful in his bold attempt to beat up the camp and rout the division of Fitzwalter; but, on the other hand, Falconbridge was sufficiently prompt to fall upon the victorious Clifford as he returned toward his main body and to efface the Yorkist disaster of the early morning by a success in the afternoon.

The same Falconbridge gave in the great battle of the ensuing day an example of the kind of tactical expedients which sufficed to decide the day when both armies were employing the same great weapon. A snowstorm, blowing against the faces of the Lancastrians, rendered the opposing lines only partially visible to each other; he therefore ordered his men to advance barely within extreme range and let fly a volley of arrows, after which he halted. The Lancastrians, finding the shafts falling among them, drew the natural conclusion that their enemies were well within range, and answered with a continuous discharge, which, since it was fired against the gale, fell short of the Yorkists by 60 yards. Half an hour of this work well-nigh exhausted their store of missiles, so that the billmen and men-of-arms of Warwick and King Edward were then able to advance without receiving any appreciable damage from the Lancastrian archery. A stratagem like this could only be used when the adversaries were perfectly conversant with each other's armament and methods of war.

That the practice of dismounting large bodies of men-at-arms, which was so prevalent on the continent in this century, was not unknown in England we have ample evidence. The Lancastrian loss at Northampton, we are told, was excessive "because the knights had sent their horses to the rear" and could not escape. Similarly, we hear of Warwick dismounting to lead a charge at Towton, and again—on certain authority—at Barnet. This custom explains the importance of the pole-ax in the knightly equipment of the fifteenth century: it was the weapon specially used by the horsemen who had descended to fight on foot. Instances of its use in this way need not be multiplied; we may, however, mention the incident which of all others seems most to have impressed the chroniclers in the fight of Edgecott Field. Sir William Herbert "valiantly acquitted himself in that, on foot and with his pole-ax in his hand, he twice by main force passed through the battle of his adversaries, and without any mortal wound returned." The engagement at which this feat of arms was performed was one notable as a renewed attempt of spearmen to stand against a mixed force of archers and cavalry. The Yorkists were utterly destitute of light troops, their bowmen having been drawn off by their commander, Lord Stafford, in a fit of pique, so that Pembroke and his North Welsh troops were left unsupported. The natural result followed: in spite of the strong position of the king's men, the rebels "by force of archery caused them quickly to descend from the hill into the valley," [20] where they were ridden down by the northern horse as they retreated in disorder.

Throughout the whole of the war artillery was in common use by both parties. Its employment was decisive at the fights of Tewkesbury and Lose-coat Field (A.D. 1470).

[20] Grafton, *op. cit.,* II, 15–16.

We also hear of it at Barnet and Northampton, as also in the sieges of the northern fortresses in 1462–1463. Its efficiency was recognized far more than that of smaller firearms, of which we find very scant mention.[21] The longbow still retained its supremacy over the arquebus, and had yet famous fields to win, notably that of Flodden, where the old maneuvers of Falkirk were repeated by both parties and the pikemen of the Lowlands were once more shot down by the archers of Cheshire and Lancashire. As late as the reign of Edward VI we find Kett's insurgents beating, by the rapidity of their archery fire, a corps of German hackbuteers whom the government had sent against them. Nor was the bow entirely extinct as a national weapon even in the days of Queen Elizabeth.

The direct influence of English methods of warfare on the general current of European military science ends with the final loss of dominion in France in the years 1450–1453. From that period the occasions of contact which had once been so frequent become rare and unimportant. The Wars of the Roses kept the English soldier at home, and after their end the pacific policy of Henry VII tended to the same result. Henry VIII exerted an influence on continental politics by diplomacy and subsidies rather than by his barren and infrequent expeditions, while in the second half of the century the peculiar characteristics of the English army of the fourteenth and fifteenth centuries had passed away, in the general change and transformation of the forms of the art of war.

[21] Edward IV is said to have had in his employment in 1470 a small corps of Germans with handguns. Better known is the band of 2,000 hackbuteers which the Earl of Lincoln brought to Stoke in 1487. The name of their leader, Martin Schwart, survives in the ballads of the day.

CHAPTER VII

Conclusion

WE HAVE now discussed at length the two systems of tactics which played the chief part in revolutionizing the art of war in Europe. The one has been traced from Morgarten to La Bicocca, the other from Falkirk to Formigny, and it has been shown how the ascendancy of each was at last checked by the development of new forms of military efficiency among those against whom it was directed. While ascribing to the pikemen of Switzerland and to the English archery the chief part in the overthrow of feudal cavalry— and to no small extent in that of feudalism itself—we must not forget that the same work was simultaneously being wrought out by other methods in other quarters of Europe.

Prominent among the experiments directed to this end was that of Jan Ziska and his captains in the great Hussite wars of the first half of the fifteenth century. In Bohemia the new military departure was the result of social and religious convulsions. A gallant nation had risen in arms, stirred at once by outraged patriotism and by spiritual zeal, moved by a desire to drive the intruding German beyond the Erzgebirge, but moved even more by dreams of universal brotherhood and of a kingdom of righteousness to be established by the sword. All Bohemia was ready to march, but still it was not apparent how the overwhelming strength of Germany was to be met. If the fate of the struggle had depended on the lances of the Czech nobility, it would have been hopeless; they could put into the field only tens to oppose to the thousands of German feudalism. The undisciplined masses of peasants and burghers who accompanied them would, under the old tactical arrangements, have fared no better than the infantry of Flanders had fared at Roosebeke. But the problem of utilizing those strong and willing arms fell into the hands of a man of genius. Jan Ziska of Trocnov had acquired military experience and hatred of Germany while fighting in the ranks of the Poles against the Teutonic knights. He saw clearly that to lead into the field men wholly untrained, and rudely armed with ironshod staves, flails, and scythes fixed to poles, would be madness. The Bohemians had neither a uniform equipment nor a national system of tactics; their only force lay in their religious and national enthusiasm, which was strong enough to make all differences vanish on the day of battle, so that the wildest fanatics were content to combine and to obey when once the foe came into sight. It was evident that the only chance for the Hussites was to stand upon the defensive till they had gauged their enemies' military efficiency and learned to handle their own arms. Accordingly we hear of entrenchments being everywhere thrown up and towns being put in a state of defense during the first months of the war. But this was not all. In his eastern campaigns Ziska had seen a military device which he thought might be developed and turned to account.

[It was a practice of the Russians to protect themselves from cavalry attacks by trains of wagons which accompanied the army on the march and which could be quickly drawn into a circle when the approach of an enemy was discovered. The Russian princes habitually utilized such a structure, which they called a *goliaigorod* or moving fortress. Ziska appropriated this system for use in mountainous Bohemia, employing at first such carts and wagons as the countryside provided, but later constructing especially designed vehicles which carried artillery and were fitted with hooks and chains by which they were fastened one to another.] [1] It was evident that these war wagons, when once placed in order, would be impregnable to a cavalry charge: however vigorous the impetus of the mailclad knight might be, it would not carry him through oaken planks and iron links. The onset of the German horseman being the chief thing which the Hussites had to dread, the battle was half won when a method of resisting it had been devised. With the German infantry they were competent to deal without any elaborate preparation.

It might be thought that Ziska's invention would have condemned the Bohemians to adhere strictly to the defensive in the whole campaign, as well as in each engagement in it; this, however, was not the case. When fully worked out, the system assumed a remarkable shape. There was organized a special corps of wagoners, on whose efficiency everything depended. They were continually drilled, and taught to maneuver their vehicles with accuracy and promptness. At the word of command, we are told, they would form a circle, a square, or a triangle, and then rapidly disengage their teams, thus leaving the wagons in proper position and only needing to be chained together. This done, they took up their position in the center of the en-

[1] For an excellent description of Hussite tactics, see Ernest Denis, *Hus et la guerre des Hussites* (Paris, 1930).

closure. The organization of the whole army was grounded on the wagon as a unit: to each was told off, besides the driver, a band of about twenty men, of whom part were pikemen and flail men, while the remainder were armed with missile weapons. The former ranged themselves behind the chains which joined wagon to wagon; the latter stood in the vehicles and fired down on the enemy. From the first Ziska set himself to introduce firearms among the Bohemians. At length nearly a third of them were armed with handguns, while a strong train of artillery accompanied every force.

A Hussite army in movement had its regular order of march. Wherever the country was open enough, the army formed five parallel columns. In the center marched the cavalry and artillery, and to each side of them two divisions of wagons accompanied by their complements of infantry. The two outer divisions were longer than the two which marched next to the horsemen and the guns. The latter were intended—in the case of a sudden attack—to form the front and rear of a great oblong, of which the longer divisions were to compose the sides. To enable the shorter columns to wheel, one forward and the other backward, no great time would be required, and if the few necessary minutes were obtained, the Hussite order of battle stood complete. To such perfection and accuracy was the execution of this maneuver brought that we are assured that a Bohemian army would march right into the middle of a German host, so as to separate division from division, and yet find time to throw itself into its normal formation just as the critical moment arrived. The only real danger was from artillery fire, which might shatter the line of carts; but the Hussites were themselves so well provided with cannon that they could usually silence the opposing batteries. Never assuredly were the tactics of the *laager* carried to such perfection; were the records of the Hussite victories not before us, we should have hesitated to believe that the Middle Ages could have produced a system whose success depended so entirely on that power of orderly movement which is usually claimed as the peculiar characteristic of modern armies. [So impressed were the historians of the fifteenth and later centuries with the efficacy of the *wagenburg* that a great deal of pure nonsense has persisted in the guise of factual history. It is impossible, for instance, that encircling movements could have been undertaken by long lines of slow-moving carts.] [2]

In the Bohemia of the fifteenth century, just as in the England of the seventeenth, fanaticism led to rigid discipline, not to disorder. The whole country, we are assured, was divided into two lists of parishes, which alternately put their entire adult population in the field. While the one half fought, the other remained at home, charged with the cultivation of their own and their neighbors' lands. A conscription law of the most sweeping kind, which made every man a soldier, was thus in force, and it becomes possible to understand the large numbers of the armies put into the field by a state of no great extent.

Ziska's first victories were to his enemies so unexpected and so marvelous that they inspired a feeling of consternation. The disproportion of numbers and the inexperience of the Hussites being taken into consideration, they were indeed surprising. But instead of abandoning their stereo-

[2] For a rational discussion of the *wagenburg* technique, see Delbrück, *Geschichte des Kriegskunst,* III, 497–519, and Oman, *Art of War,* II, 361–370.

typed feudal tactics, to whose inability to cope with any new form of military efficiency the defeats were really due, the Germans merely tried to raise larger armies, and sent them to incur the same fate as the first host which Sigismund had led against Prague. But the engagements only grew more decisive as Ziska fully developed his tactical methods. Invasion after invasion was a failure because, when once the Bohemians came in sight, the German leaders could not induce their troops to stand firm. The men utterly declined to face the flails and pikes of their enemies, even when the latter advanced far beyond their rampart of wagons and assumed the offensive. The Hussites were consequently so exalted with the confidence of their own invincibility that they undertook, and often successfully carried out, actions of the most extraordinary temerity. Relying on the terror which they inspired, small bodies would attack superior numbers when every military consideration was against them, and yet would win the day. Bands only a few thousand strong sallied forth from the natural fortress formed by the Bohemian mountains and wasted Bavaria, Meissen, Thuringia, and Silesia, almost without hindrance. They returned in safety, their war wagons laden with the spoil of eastern Germany, and leaving a broad track of desolation behind them. Long after Ziska's death the prestige of his tactics remained undiminished, and his successors were able to accomplish feats of war which would have appeared incredible in the first years of the war.

When at last the defeat of the Taborites took place, it resulted from the dissensions of the Bohemians themselves, not from the increased efficiency of their enemies. The battle of Lipan (May 30, 1434), where Procopius fell and the

extreme party were crushed, was a victory won not by the
Germans but by the more moderate sections of the Czech
nation. The event of the fight indicates at once the weak
spot of Hussite tactics and the tremendous self-confidence
of the Taborites. After Procopius had repelled the first assaults on his circle of wagons, his men—forgetting that
they had to do not with the panic-stricken hosts of their
old enemies but with their own former comrades,—left
their defenses and charged the retreating masses. They
were accustomed to see the maneuver succeed against the
terrorized Germans, and forgot that it was only good when
turned against adversaries whose spirit was entirely broken.
In itself an advance meant the sacrifice of all the benefits
of a system of tactics which was essentially defensive. The
weakness, in fact, of the device of the wagon fortress was
that, although securing the repulse of the enemy, it gave
no opportunity for following up that success if he was wary
and retreated in good order. This, however, was not a re-
proach to the inventor of the system, for Ziska had originally to seek not for the way to win decisive victories, but
for the way to avoid crushing defeats. At Lipan the moderate party had been beaten back but not routed. Accordingly, when the Taborites came out into the open field, the
retreating masses turned to fight, while a cavalry reserve
which far outnumbered the horsemen of Procopius rode
in between the circle of wagons and the troops which had
left it. Thus three-quarters of the Taborite army were
caught and surrounded in the plain, where they were cut
to pieces by the superior numbers of the enemy. Only the
few thousands who had remained behind within the wagon
fortress succeeded in escaping. Thus was demonstrated the
incompleteness for military purposes of a system which had

been devised as a political necessity, not as an infallible recipe for victory.

The moral of the fight of Lipan was indeed the same as the moral of the fight of Hastings. Purely defensive tactics are hopeless when opposed by a commander of ability and resource who is provided with steady troops. If the German princes had been generals and the German troops well-disciplined, the careers of Ziska and Procopius would have been impossible. Bad strategy and panic combined to make the Hussites seem invincible. When, however, they were met by rational tactics they were found to be no less liable to the logic of war than were other men.

Long before the flails and handguns of Ziska's infantry had turned to rout the chivalry of Germany, another body of foot soldiers had won the respect of eastern Europe. On the battlefields of the Balkan Peninsula the Slav and the Magyar had learned to dread the slave soldiery of the Ottoman sultans.

Authorities are unanimous in crediting the sultan Orkhan with the creation of the corps of Janizaries, but there is no positive evidence that they formed an important element in the Ottoman armies much before the beginning of the fifteenth century. The victories at Kossovo (1389) and Nicopolis (1396) were won by the heavily mailed spahis of the guard; at the latter battle, the charge of the Serbian knights of Stephan Lazarevic contributed considerably to the defeat of Sigismund. Not until the time of Suleiman the Magnificent were the Janizaries recruited up to a strength of 12,000. They owed their early successes to precisely the same causes as did the English archer. This early weapon was the bow, not indeed the longbow of the West, but nevertheless a very efficient arm. The rest of the

Janizary's equipment was very simple: he carried no defensive arms, and wore only a pointed felt cap and a flowing gray tunic reaching to his knees. Besides his bow and quiver, he was armed with a scimitar and a long knife. Though disciplined fanaticism made them formidable foes in close combat, it was not for that kind of fighting that the Janizaries were designed. When we find them storming a trench or leading a charge, they were going beyond their own province. Their entire want of armor alone would have sufficed to show that they were not designed for hand-to-hand contests, and it is a noteworthy fact that they could never be induced to take to the use of the pike. Like the English archery, they were used either in defensive positions or to supplement the employment of cavalry. But the Turkish armies of the late fourteenth century were composed chiefly of the timariot cavalry—based upon an Oriental variation of fief-holding—who not only operated as horse archers, but were armed with the spear, and are often mentioned as fighting in close combat with mace and saber. In addition, there was a solid core composed of the heavily mailed cavalry—the spahis—of the sultan's guard and the small regular unit of infantry of the Janizaries. These were augmented in time of war by irregular auxiliaries, light troops both infantry and cavalry, useful as scouts and skirmishers. This was the military organization which overran the Balkan Peninsula as far as the line of the Danube and the Save in the fourteenth and fifteenth centuries.[3]

[It was successful chiefly because of the disunity of its opponents. The most formidable enemy of the Ottoman sultans was Hungary, whose kings were more interested

[3] This paragraph and the one which follows it have been rewritten by the editor.

in bringing the Serbians and Bulgarians to Roman Catholicism than in uniting all of Balkan Christendom against the Turk. And the elevation of King Sigismund to the imperial throne caused that energetic monarch to devote most of his time to German and papal, rather than Balkan, affairs. Only the appearance of two great leaders in the second half of the fifteenth century—John Huniades (1444–1456) and his son, Matthias Corvinus (1458–1490) —enabled the Hungarians to hold the line of the Danube. The military organization of Hungary was eminently suited for coping with the Turks. Of all the European nations, Hungary alone possessed a national force of horse archers. The archers, added to the feudal magnates who had adopted western feudal arms, produced a combination which paralleled the Ottoman bow and lance. By the middle of the fifteenth century, however, the Hungarians, who had no native infantry, occasionally hired European mercenaries— pikemen and hackbuteers, chiefly—to supply this deficiency, which was probably emphasized by the increasing numbers of Janizaries in the Turkish armies.]

For this reason the most interesting of Ottoman fights from the tactician's point of view was the second battle of Kossovo (1449). This was not—like Varna (A.D. 1444) or Mohács (A.D. 1526)—an ill-advised attempt to break the Turkish line by a headlong onset. John Huniades, whom long experience had made familiar with the tactics of his enemy, endeavored to turn against Sultan Murad his own usual scheme. To face the Janizaries he drew up in his center a strong force of German infantry armed with the handguns whose use the Hussites had introduced. On the wings the chivalry of Hungary were destined to cope with the masses of the timariot cavalry. In consequence of this arrangement, the two centers faced each other for long hours, neither advancing, but each occupied in thinning the enemy's ranks, the one with the arbalest bolt, the other with the bullet. Meanwhile, on the wings' desperate cavalry charges succeeded each other, till on the second day the Walachian allies of Huniades gave way before the superior numbers of the Ottomans and the Christian center had to draw off and retire. So desperate had the fighting been that half the Hungarian army and a third of that of Murad was left upon the field. The tactical meaning of the engagement was plain: good infantry could make a long resistance to the Ottoman arms, even if they could not secure the victory. The lesson, however, was not fully realized, and it was not till the military revolution of the sixteenth century that infantry was destined to take the prominent part in withstanding the Ottoman. The *Landsknechte* and hackbuteers of Charles V and Ferdinand of Austria proved much more formidable foes to the sultans than the gallant but undisciplined light cavalry [4] of Hungary. This was to a great extent due to the perfection of pike tactics in the west. The Turks, whose infantry could never be induced to adopt that weapon,[5] relied entirely on their firearms, and were checked by the combination of pike and hackbut.

It is noticeable that the Janizaries took to the use of the firelock at a comparatively early date. It may have been in consequence of the effectiveness of Huniades' handguns at Kossovo that we find them discarding the arbalest in favor

[4] Already since the middle of the fifteenth century known as "Hussars."

[5] Montecuculi notes that even in his day, far into the seventeenth century, the Turk had not yet taken to the pike (Raimondo de Montecuculi, *Mémoires* [Amsterdam, 1752], p. 236).

of the newer weapon. But at any rate the Ottoman had fully accomplished the change long before it had been finally carried out in Europe and nearly a century earlier than the nations of the further East.[6]

In recognizing the full importance of cannon, the sultans were equally in advance of their times. The capture of Constantinople by Mahomet II was probably the first event of supreme importance whose result was determined by the power of artillery. The lighter guns of previous years had never accomplished any feat comparable in its results to that which was achieved by the siege train of the Conqueror. Some decades later we find the Janizaries' line of arquebuses supported by the fire of fieldpieces, often brought forward in great numbers and chained together so as to prevent cavalry from charging down the intervals between the guns.[7] This device is said to have been employed with great success against an enemy superior in the numbers of his horsemen, alike at Dolbek (A.D. 1516) and at Chaldiran (A.D. 1514).

The ascendancy of the Turkish arms was finally terminated by the conjunction of several causes. Of these the chief was the rise in central Europe of standing armies composed for the most part of disciplined infantry. But it is no less undoubted that much was due to the fact that the Ottomans after the reign of Suleiman fell behind their contemporaries in readiness to keep up with the advance of military skill, a change which may be connected with

[6] The arquebus and cannon were novelties to the Mamelukes as late as 1517, if we are to trust the story of Kait Bey.

[7] Richard III of England is said to have adopted this expedient at Bosworth.

the gradual transformation of the Janizaries from a corps into a caste. It should also be remembered that the frontier of Christendom was now covered not by one isolated fortress of supreme importance, such as Belgrade had been, but by a double and triple line of strong towns whose existence made it hard for the Turks to advance with rapidity or to reap any such results from success in a single battle or siege as had been possible in the previous century.

On the warfare of the other nations of eastern Europe it will not be necessary to dwell. The military history of Russia, though interesting in itself, exercised no influence on the general progress of the art of war. With the more important development of new tactical methods in southwestern Europe we have already dealt when describing the Spanish infantry in the chapter devoted to the Swiss and their enemies.

All the systems of real weight and consideration have been discussed. In the overthrow of the supremacy of feudal cavalry the tactics of the shock and the tactics of the missile had each played their part; which had been the more effective it would be hard to say. Between them, however, the task had been successfully accomplished. The military strength of that system which had embraced all Europe in its cramping fetters had been shattered to atoms. Warlike efficiency was the attribute no longer of a class but of whole nations, and war had ceased to be an occupation in which feudal chivalry found its pleasure and the rest of society its ruin. The art of war had become once more a living reality, a matter not of tradition but of experiment, and the vigorous sixteenth century was rapidly adding to it new forms and variations. The Middle Ages were at last over, and the stirring and scientific spirit of the modern world was working a transformation in military matters which was to make the methods of mediaeval war seem even further removed from the strategy of our own century than are the operations of the ancients in the great days of Greece and Rome.

Chronological List of Battles

Bouvines	27 July 1214
Taillebourg	20 July 1242
El Mansûra	8 February 1250
Kressenbrunn	1260
Lewes	14 May 1264
Evesham	4 August 1265
Benevento	26 February 1266
Tagliacozzo	23 August 1268
Orwin Bridge	11 December 1282
Conway, near	22 January 1295
Hasenbühl	1298
Falkirk	22 July 1298
Courtrai	11 July 1302
Mons-en-Pévèle	18 August 1304
Bannockburn	24 June 1314
Morgarten	15 November 1315
Cassel	1328
Halidon Hill	19 July 1333
Laupen	21 June 1339
Crécy	26 August 1346
Neville's Cross	17 October 1346
Poitiers	19 September 1356
Auray	29 September 1364
Roosebeke	27 November 1382
Aljubarrota	14 August 1385
Sempach	9 July 1386
Kossovo I	15 June 1389
Nicopolis	25 September 1396
Homildon	14 September 1402
Agincourt	25 October 1415
Arbedo	30 June 1422
Cravant	31 July 1423
Verneuil	17 August 1424
Herrings, Day of	12 February 1429

Patay	19 June 1429
Lipan	16 June 1434
St. Jacob-en-Birs	24 August 1444
Varna	10 November 1444
Kossovo II	17 October 1449
Formigny	15 April 1450
Constantinople, siege of	April–May 1453
Castillon	17 July 1453
St. Albans I	22 April 1455
Blore Heath	22 September 1459
Northampton	18 July 1460
Towton	29 March 1461
Hedgeley Moor	25 April 1464
Waldshut, siege of	1468
Edgecott Field	26 July 1469
Lose-Coat Field	1470
Barnet	14 April 1471
Tewkesbury	4 May 1471
Grandson	2 March 1476
Morat	22 June 1476
Nancy	5 January 1477
Dornach	1499
Frastenz	1499
Barletta	1503
Genoa, storm of	1507
Ravenna	11 April 1512
Novara	6 June 1513
Flodden	9 September 1513
Chaldiran	23 August 1514
Marignano	15 September 1515
Dolbek	24 August 1516
La Bicocca	27 April 1522
Pavia	21 February 1525
Mohacs	29 August 1526

Index